MONOLOGUES
FROM THE CLASSICS

LAMDA
MONOLOGUES
FROM THE CLASSICS

Edited by Shaun McKenna

PUBLISHED BY
OBERON BOOKS
FOR THE LONDON ACADEMY OF
MUSIC AND DRAMATIC ART

First published in 2004 for LAMDA Ltd. by Oberon Books Ltd.
(incorporating Absolute Classics)
521 Caledonian Road, London N7 9RH
Tel: 020 7607 3637 / Fax: 020 7607 3629
e-mail: oberon.books@btinternet.com
www.oberonbooks.com

A catalogue record for this book is available from the British Library.

ISBN 1 84002 422 4

Cover design: Joe Ewart

Photograph: John Haynes

Printed in Great Britain by Antony Rowe Ltd, Chippenham.

Contents

II: FEMALE MONOLOGUES

Introduction

Monologues from the Classics contains a collection of solo speeches for men and women taken from sixteen of the most significant playwrights of the last three millennia.

The speeches have been chosen to be approachable by performers from their mid-teens upwards. Some are clearly more difficult than others and length should not be confused with complexity – some of the shorter speeches are every bit as challenging as the lengthier ones. Playing time ranges from around two-and-a-half minutes to approximately five minutes, though some of the longer speeches can be cut to a variety of lengths depending on the demands of the occasion.

Though the speeches are selected to be suitable for younger actors, this by no means implies that all the characters fall into this age range. Certainly, there is plenty of youthful passion to be found here, but there are also terrific character roles which an adept and ambitious young actor can realistically hope to bring to three-dimensional life. The range of styles is wide, from the bleakest tragedy to the broadest farce and not always from the authors one expects.

One of the pleasures of compiling an anthology of this kind is the discovery (or rediscovery) of great but little-known plays. There are always hundreds of plays that one intends to read 'when there is time'. The list of authors set by LAMDA Examinations for its Advanced Level selections allowed me to explore many forgotten works (amazing the riches that a complete edition of say Wycherley and Behn throws up!) and undisputed masterpieces, to discover the best and most appropriate moments for performance. I felt it was as important to include well-known solo speeches as it was to unearth less familiar choices. The famous speeches are often famous for good reason and sometimes looking at them in unfamiliar company brings new insights.

I have chosen not to omit the dialogue of other characters but to include the full text and author's stage directions. Sections which should be omitted in performance, to ensure the smooth development of a solo performance, have been set inside square brackets. In the case of translations, I have given the ISBN of the version used. Editions of English language plays are readily available.

Restoration period texts have been slightly 'interfered with', it being my belief that the preponderance of capital letters for all nouns is off-putting to the reader. Of the many different editions of Shakespeare, I have chosen to follow the punctuation of the Arden edition. I have provided footnotes where a meaning or reference seems obscure to me, but I hope I have not been over-zealous in providing explanatory notes. The Appendix contains brief biographical details of each of the playwrights. Each speech has a brief introduction outlining both the character and the situation. These will provide useful context when making selections but should not be regarded as a substitute for reading the play.

I hope this collection proves as enjoyable to read as it was to compile.

Shaun McKenna

I: MALE MONOLOGUES

ANTIGONE (442 BC)

by Sophocles
English version by Declan Donnellan

PUBLISHED BY OBERON BOOKS (ISBN 1 84002 136 5)

The two sons of the banished King Oedipus led a failed rebellion against the tyrannical Creon, King of Thebes. Both were killed and Creon has given orders that their bodies should remain unburied. In Greek terms, this means that they cannot pass on to the afterlife. However, their sister Antigone has defied the ban and scattered earth on their bodies. Creon's decree is that Antigone must die as punishment for defying his order. HAEMON, Creon's son, is in love with Antigone. Here he argues with his father.

HAEMON: Father, the Gods sow intelligence in men,
    The greatest of all their gifts, and you know
    That I could never say that you were wrong
    And may I never learn how to suggest
    Such a thing. But, Father, you cannot hear
    What Thebes is yet to say. The man in the street
    Quakes when disapproval narrows your eyes.
    What I am trying to say is this: sometimes
    It's easier for me to hear the darkness
    Whispering and preparing to whisper
    How this girl will be mourned, how Thebes will feel,
    To see that head smashed by a shower of stones.
    How they will say a coronet of gold
    Would better suit those eyes that would not see
    Her brother's corpse exposed to tooth of dog.
    This shadowy talk has crept to my ears.

Your prosperity is my happiness.
The son enjoys to hear his father praised.
No greater joy can beat a father's heart
Than when his child is loved. Let me love you,
Father. Hear me when I ask you to hear
Another point of view. You must not think
You own the monopoly of wisdom;
Whoever thinks that he alone has sense
Rings hollow as a drum. Wisdom knows that she
Has much to learn and clasps the new idea
As her most honoured guest. This is why, Father,
When winter hurls the river down the hills
To burst its puny banks, it is the trees
That yield with grace which manage to survive,
But the mighty oak, too proud to bend, is ripped
From his deep roots and tossed into the roar.
The captain needs humility to see
His tiny boat is weaker than the storm.
A sail too tight will whip him upside down:
Round rolls the canvas; captain, planks and all
Plummet to eternity. No, father – think,
Feel your anger but do not act on it.
I know that I am young but I say this:
No-one knows everything.

ANTIGONE (442 BC)

by Sophocles
English version by Declan Donnellan

PUBLISHED BY OBERON BOOKS (ISBN 1 84002 136 5)

The two sons of the banished King Oedipus led a failed rebellion against Creon, King of Thebes, and both were killed. Creon ordered that their bodies remain unburied but Antigone, the sister of the dead men, insisted on burying them. In defying Creon, Antigone was condemned to death. Creon's son, Haemon, supported Antigone and contradicted his father's orders. Here, the MESSENGER describes how this tragic saga came to an end.

MESSENGER: Dear mistress. I was there. I saw it all
    And I will spare no detail. Why should I
    Comfort you with lies? The truth is always right.
    I ran behind your husband to the plain
    Where Polynices stretched his lifeless limbs.
    We knelt and prayed to pacify the Gods,
    Begging Pluto to restrain his deep rage.
    We washed the body with holy water,
    Burnt the remains in a fresh pyre and heaped
    A funeral mound of his native earth.
    We turned towards his sister's living tomb,
    Her bridal bed of darkness and damp stone.
    We thought we heard a cry within the tomb
    And ran to tell our master. We approached.
    Moaning and keening echoed round the rocks.
    Creon froze, 'Oh, miserable man,' he cried,
    'Is it only now I see the future?

I was always cautious, always prudent,
Saw the path to ruin, took another way.
But have I run in one almighty circle?
Is that my son I hear? I cannot see.
Is Haemon in the tomb or am I mad?'
We peered within and scrambled down and this
Is what we saw: at the far end it was:
In and out of the shadows she drifted,
Turning on a noose of linen thread.
Lying close, steadying her, was Haemon,
Howling and howling uncontrollably
His ruined marriage, and his father's sins.
Creon cried out and ran towards his son,
Beseeching, 'Oh my child, what have you done?
What would you do? You have been driven mad.
Come out and be my son again, I beg!'
But the boy glared at him with those wild eyes,
Spat in his father's face and in a flash
Drew his two-edged sword. Out ran the father
And the son missed. His blind lurching rage he
Turned within and deep into his own heart
Plunged the glinting steel. With Haemon's last breaths
He tried to still and fix Antigone
But his arms were weak and his last quick gasps
Splattered drops of blood across her cheeks.
And so they rocked together in their bed,
And Hades blessed their union with silence.
What greater evil can befall a man
Than to act before he has time to think?

MEDEA

by Euripides (431 BC)
Translated by Alistair Elliot

PUBLISHED BY OBERON BOOKS (ISBN 1 870259 36 X)

Medea helped the hero JASON to defeat her father, the King of Colchis, so JASON married her and she bore him two children. Returned to his home town of Thebes, JASON finds himself a hero and is offered the hand in marriage of the King's daughter. To make this possible, he must divorce and abandon Medea, who will be banished from Thebes. Medea reacts violently to this news. Here, JASON comes to speak with her and refutes her suggestion that he owes his status as a hero to her.

JASON: You greatly exaggerate your kind assistance.
　　You claim you saved the Argo expedition.
　　I have to say I credit Aphrodite
　　And only Aphrodite, no-one else.
　　You have quick wits, so it's not necessary –
　　Indeed it would be indelicate and ungrateful
　　To list the many ways in which Desire,
　　Drove you, helpless, on to save my life.
　　So I shan't press the point in any detail;
　　I grant you helped me, and I'm glad you did.
　　On the other hand, you got more than you gave.
　　The first thing is, you live in Greece, instead
　　Of somewhere barbarous; you have learned of justice,
　　To enjoy the rule of law – not the whim of despots.
　　Then, all the Greeks have heard of you, the wise one,
　　And you are famous; if you were still living
　　At the edge of the world, there'd be no talk of you.

For me, I wouldn't want a houseful of gold,
Or a finer singing voice than Orpheus –
Unless mankind could hear and point me out.

(I've said that much about the Labours of Jason
Only because you put the subject forward.)
You also reproach me for my royal marriage:
I'm going to show you that was well thought out,
Entirely prudent, not a mindless impulse:
I was acting as the greatest possible friend
For you, and for my children – just keep calm.

When I moved on from Iolcos and came here,
Dragging misfortune inescapably
Behind me, what better treasure-trove could I have found
Than marriage with the daughter of a king – I, an exile?
Now don't torment yourself: don't think I'm weary
Of your bed; or that I'm smitten with desire
For a fresh wife – or have some strange ambition
To rival others who have many children –
Those that I have suffice – I've no complaint – of
                                        them or you.

I acted solely to ensure that we live well
And never go without, because I know
People will shun a man who's lost his wealth.
Also, I hoped to bring my children up
In a manner worthy of my own descent;
I thought I'd breed some brothers for our sons,
Make them all equal, bring our lines together.
That way our happiness and security lies.
You don't need children – you have had enough –
But I could make my sons to come be useful
To those that I have now – is that a bad ambition?

You would approve – except that the marriage irks you.
Isn't that like a woman? You believe

While bed is right that everything is right,
But if you're left alone between the sheets
You treat your nearest, dearest and best friend
As your worst enemy. We should make our children
Some other way – and have no breed of women.
Then we would live as happy as the gods.

AJAX (c 410 BC)

by Sophocles
Translated by James Kerr

PUBLISHED BY OBERON BOOKS (ISBN 1 84002 105 5)

AJAX is the King of Salamis and, after Achilles, the bravest of the key figures in the Greek camp laying siege to Troy. After the death of Achilles, AJAX and Odysseus fight for the dead hero's weapons. When they are allotted to Odysseus, AJAX goes mad with rage. In this scene, already deranged, AJAX tells the Chorus of his despair as he struggles to see a way forward for himself.

AJAX: Ajax
 All that I am is my name
 There is no more to say

 (*He lets out a cry which sounds like his name.*)

 My father fought here
 And came home the army's choice
 I followed
 Hero son of a hero
 And now my honour dies with me
 Yet so much I think I know
 That if Achilles were alive and here today
 If Achilles himself were able to award
 His own armour, a prize for valour
 There would have been only one result
 A victory for Ajax
 But the sons of Atreus forgot my name
 Forgot about the army's choice
 When they handed them to Odysseus

For what? …Well? …for what?
I dreamed on and on of bloody Justice
Flattered by my own visions
But I now see my mind was blind
The Savage Goddess poisoned my eyes
And stained my sword with the blood of beasts
No more than a trick, a simple trick
Even a coward can win with a little help
And now I'm hated
Hated by the gods, my army
Troy, and these war-fields
Where now then?
Could I return home?
Desert my ships, leave the battle
Let the sons of Atreus tremble alone
Home to my father, my great father
How can I look at you now?
Shall I smile when you lift my face
You'd condemn me with pity
It is not possible
Should I walk alone to the wall of Troy
Fight each damned Trojan till I am dead
Praised and buried by Greek enemies
It is not possible
My father, I will find a way
My only hope is in death's mercy
All I am in life is shame
There is nothing else
Day follows day, there is nothing else

BACCHAI (406 BC)

by Euripides
Translated by Colin Teevan

PUBLISHED BY OBERON BOOKS (ISBN 1 84002 261 2)

Euripides' last play is a violent tragedy about the power of ecstasy and the release of inhibitions. PENTHEUS, King of Thebes, is arrogant and dismissive of the power of the gods. The god Dionysus, disguised as a human, has arrived in Thebes and taught the women of the city to worship him. PENTHEUS is angry and scandalised by the excesses of the god's devotees.

PENTHEUS: I leave the city for three short days
    And am no sooner on the road but hear
    That all our women have abandoned house and home
    And taken to the mountains in nothing
    But the skins of beasts and gad about
    Dark forests in demented dancing,
    In the name of some new-fangled cult
    Of Dionysus. Furthermore I hear
    The chief practice of this cult consists
    Of drinking quantities of wine then sneaking
    Off to slake the thirsts of male concelebrants.
    They might see this as some sort of sacred rite
    Of this self-styled god, but from what I see
    They are driven not by duty but desire.
    Those whom I've caught I've bound both hand and foot
    And placed under heavy guard in prison,
    Those who remain at large I will hunt down.
    That includes Agave, my own mother,
    Her sisters Ino and Autonoe,
    Mother of my dead cousin Actaeon.

With hunter's net and manacles of iron,
I will stop these evil rites from spreading.
I've also heard that some Asian foreigner,
Masquerading as a kind of priest,
With big brown eyes and long, golden hair
– Too womanish to be a proper man –
Keeps constant company with our women
And with his song and dance leads them astray.
If I catch him within my city's walls
I'd soon stop his drumstick drumming
I'll cut off those long, gold, blond locks of his.
He's the one who claims that Dionysus
Is a god hatched from the thigh of Zeus.
Dionysus is no god, nor son of god
But died in the womb in the lightning blast
That killed his mother, my aunt, Semele;
Struck down for the boast that she'd lain with Zeus.
The gods will always punish arrogance.
And this foreigner, like Semele, will pay.
And what's this? Another wonder! Our prophet
Teiresias dressed in the dappled deerskin
And grandfather with a wand of ivy?
Has the whole city gone completely mad?
You make me sick, you make me want to laugh.
You make me want to laugh till I throw up.
So many years and yet so little sense.
Take off that wreath of ivy grandfather!
Throw down that silly stick! Do what I say!
I blame you for all of this Teiresias,
You hope by the invention of new gods
To expand your business in burnt offerings.
If it weren't for your wrinkles and grey hair
I'd bind you like the women, hand and foot,
For spreading such unseemly practices.

PHILOCTETES (c 405 BC)

by Sophocles
Translated by Keith Dewhurst

PUBLISHED BY OBERON BOOKS (ISBN 1 870259 93 9)

The Trojan war has been going on for ten long years and the Greeks, who are laying siege to Troy, need all the help they can get. The great Greek hero, Achilles, is dead. The wily, cunning general Odysseus has brought Achilles' son, NEOPTOLEMUS, to a deserted island, in order to obtain the magical bow which belongs to Philoctetes. Philoctetes is an old man, the arch-enemy of Odysseus. He is hideously injured with a wound that never heals, and has become a recluse on this distant island. It is NEOPTOLEMUS' task to use all his powers of persuasion to make Philoctetes give up the magic bow – it has been foretold that it will be decisive in assuring a Greek victory. Here, NEOPTOLEMUS tells Philoctetes a pack of lies as persuasively as he can.

NEOPTOLEMUS: Odysseus and my father's old tutor came for me in a decorated galley. They said, perhaps truly or perhaps falsely, that because of what the gods had brought to pass, the death of my father, only I could take the citadel of Troy. Sir, when they said this I did not waste time. I sailed with them – mostly because I longed to see before his burial the father I had never known in life. But also, I admit, because of the promise that I should capture Troy. We had a favourable wind, and on the second day reached Sigeum. As I went ashore the host encircled me and blessed me, and swore I was Achilles come to life

again. But he had left them forever. I mourned him,
and when some time had passed went to Agamemnon
and Menelaus as my close friends, and claimed my
father's goods and weapons. Their answer was
impudence itself: 'Son of Achilles, all that your father
owned indeed belongs to you, except his weapons,
which now belong to Odysseus.' I wept. I started up
in grievous anger and I harangued them. 'You rogues,
how dare you give my arms to someone else before I
knew of it?' Then Odysseus, who stood near me, said,
'Yes, boy, and they gave them justly, because I
recaptured both the weapons and the body.' I burst
into a passionate rage. I used all kinds of curses on the
man who took away my arms. He is slow to anger, but
he was stung and burst out, 'For all your fine words
you were nowhere near us. You'll never sail to Skyros
with my weapons!' So the insults flew and I sailed
homewards, robbed by Odysseus, the vilest son of vile
parents. Yet he is less to blame than the generals: an
army, like a state, is under authority, and men act badly
because their leaders teach them to do so. That's my
story. May whoever hates the generals be as dear to
the gods as he is to me!

KING JOHN (c 1592)

by William Shakespeare

The heroic BASTARD OF FAULCONBRIDGE manifests wit, courage and gallantry as he fights for right against the machinations of the weak and wicked King John. Prince Arthur was heir to the throne and was in the safe-keeping of Hubert. It was in King John's interests that Arthur should die, though Hubert could not bring himself to kill the boy. Arthur, in fact, has committed suicide by throwing himself from the battlements. Here the BASTARD demands an explanation from Hubert.

Act IV, Scene III

BASTARD: Here's a good world! Knew you of this fair
work?
    Beyond the infinite and boundless reach
    Of mercy, if thou didst this deed of death,
    Art thou damn'd, Hubert.

[HUBERT: Do but hear me, sir.]

BASTARD: Ha! I'll tell thee what;
    Thou'rt damn'd as black – nay, nothing is so black;
    Thou art more deep damn'd than Prince Lucifer:
    There is not yet so ugly a fiend of hell
    As thou shalt be, if thou didst kill this child.

[HUBERT: Upon my soul –]

BASTARD: If thou didst but consent
    To this most cruel act, do but despair;
    And if thou want'st a cord, the smallest thread
    That ever spider twisted from her womb

Will serve to strangle thee, a rush will be a beam
To hang thee on; or wouldst thou drown thyself,
Put but a little water in a spoon,
And it shall be as all the ocean,
Enough to stifle such a villain up.
I do suspect thee very grievously.

[HUBERT: If I in act, consent, or sin of thought,
Be guilty of the stealing that sweet breath
Which was embounded in this beauteous clay,
Let hell want pains enough to torture me.
I left him well.]

BASTARD: Go, bear him in thine arms.
I am amazed, methinks, and lose my way
Among the thorns and dangers of this world.
How easy dost thou take all England up!
From forth this morsel of dead royalty,
The life, the right and truth of all this realm
Is fled to heaven; and England now is left
To tug and scramble and to part by the teeth
The unowed interest of proud-swelling state.
Now for the bare-pick'd bone of majesty
Doth dogged war bristle his angry crest
And snarleth in the gentle eyes of peace:
Now powers from home and discontents at home
Meet in one line; and vast confusion waits,
As doth a raven on a sick-fall'n beast,
The imminent decay of wrested pomp.
Now happy he whose cloak and cincture can
Hold out this tempest. Bear away that child
And follow me with speed: I'll to the king:
A thousand businesses are brief in hand,
And heaven itself doth frown upon the land.

(*Exeunt.*)

HENRY VI PART 3 (c 1592)

by William Shakespeare

In the bloody chaos and civil war which characterised the Wars of the Roses, the handsome Edward IV has become King, thanks to the help of his brothers RICHARD OF GLOUCESTER and George of Clarence. RICHARD OF GLOUCESTER, in Shakespeare's version, is a hunch-backed, twisted, evil and ambitious monster who wants the crown of England for himself and who will stop at nothing to get it. He will eventually become Richard III and this great speech, one of the earliest of Shakespeare's major soliloquies, is reminiscent of the more celebrated 'Now is the winter of our discontent' speech which opens Richard III.

Act III, Scene II

GLOUCESTER: Ay, Edward will use women honourably.
    Would he were wasted, marrow, bones and all,
    That from his loins no hopeful branch may spring,
    To cross me from the golden time I look for!
    And yet, between my soul's desire and me –
    The lustful Edward's title buried –
    Is Clarence, Henry, and his son young Edward,
    And all the unlook'd for issue of their bodies,
    To take their rooms, ere I can place myself:
    A cold premeditation for my purpose!
    Why, then, I do but dream on sovereignty;
    Like one that stands upon a promontory,
    And spies a far-off shore where he would tread,
    Wishing his foot were equal with his eye,
    And chides the sea that sunders him from thence,

Saying, he'll lade it dry to have his way:
So do I wish the crown, being so far off;
And so I chide the means that keeps me from it;
And so I say, I'll cut the causes off,
Flattering me with impossibilities.
My eye's too quick, my heart o'erweens too much,
Unless my hand and strength could equal them.
Well, say there is no kingdom then for Richard;
What other pleasure can the world afford?
I'll make my heaven in a lady's lap,
And deck my body in gay ornaments,
And witch sweet ladies with my words and looks.
O miserable thought! and more unlikely
Than to accomplish twenty golden crowns!
Why, love forswore me in my mother's womb:
And, for I should not deal in her soft laws,
She did corrupt frail nature with some bribe,
To shrink mine arm up like a wither'd shrub;
To make an envious mountain on my back,
Where sits deformity to mock my body;
To shape my legs of an unequal size;
To disproportion me in every part,
Like to a chaos, or an unlick'd bear-whelp
That carries no impression like the dam.
And am I then a man to be beloved?
O monstrous fault, to harbour such a thought!
Then, since this earth affords no joy to me,
But to command, to check, to o'erbear such
As are of better person than myself,
I'll make my heaven to dream upon the crown,
And, whiles I live, to account this world but hell,
Until my mis-shaped trunk that bears this head
Be round impaled with a glorious crown.
And yet I know not how to get the crown,

For many lives stand between me and home:
And I, – like one lost in a thorny wood,
That rends the thorns and is rent with the thorns,
Seeking a way and straying from the way;
Not knowing how to find the open air,
But toiling desperately to find it out, –
Torment myself to catch the English crown:
And from that torment I will free myself,
Or hew my way out with a bloody axe.
Why, I can smile, and murder whiles I smile,
And cry 'Content' to that which grieves my heart,
And wet my cheeks with artificial tears,
And frame my face to all occasions.
I'll drown more sailors than the mermaid shall;
I'll slay more gazers than the basilisk;
I'll play the orator as well as Nestor,
Deceive more slily than Ulysses could,
And, like a Sinon, take another Troy.
I can add colours to the chameleon,
Change shapes with Proteus for advantages,
And set the murderous Machiavel to school.
Can I do this, and cannot get a crown?
Tut, were it farther off, I'll pluck it down.

(*Exit.*)

THE WHITE DEVIL (1608)

by John Webster

This violent tragedy, based on fact, tells the story of Vittoria Corombona, who becomes the mistress of the Duke of Brachiano. FLAMINEO, Vittoria's brother, helps the Duke to corrupt Vittoria and to murder her husband. Later, FLAMINEO kills his own brother, Marcello, and watches his distracted mother, Cornelia, go mad with grief. In this scene, FLAMINEO has a change of heart and sees the ghost of the now-murdered Brachiano.

Act V, Scene V

FLAMINEO: I have a strange thing in me, to the which
    I cannot give a name, without it be
    Compassion; I pray leave me.   (*Exit Francisco.*)
    This night I'll know the utmost of my fate,
    I'll be resolv'd what my rich sister means
    T'assign me for my service. I have liv'd
    Riotously ill, like some that live in court.
    And sometimes, when my face was full of smiles
    Have felt the maze of conscience in my breast.
    Oft gay and honour'd robes those tortures try,
    We think cag'd birds sing, when indeed they cry.

    (*Enter Brachiano's Ghost. In his leather cassock and breeches, boots, a cowl [and in his hand] a pot of lily-flowers with a skull in't.*)

    Ha! I can stand thee. Nearer, nearer yet.
    What a mockery hath death made of thee? Thou
                        look'st sad.
    In what place art thou? in yon starry gallery,

Or in the cursed dungeon? No? not speak?
Pray, sir, resolve me, what religion's best
For a man to die in? or is it in your knowledge
To answer me how long I have to live?
That's the most necessary question.
Not answer? Are you still like some great men
That only walk like shadows up and down,
And to no purpose: say: —

(*The ghost throws earth upon him and shows him the skull.*)

What's that? O fatal! He throws earth upon me.
A dead man's skull beneath the roots of flowers.
I pray speak sir; our Italian churchmen
Make us believe, dead men hold conference
With their familiars, and many times
Will come to bed to them, and eat with them. (*Exit Ghost.*)
He's gone; and see, the skull and earth are vanish'd.
This is beyond melancholy. I do dare my fate
To do its worst. Now to my sister's lodging,
And sum up all these horrors; the disgrace
The Prince threw on me; next the piteous sight
Of my dead brother; and my mother's dotage;
And last this terrible vision. All these
Shall with Vittoria's bounty turn to good,
Or I will drown this weapon in her blood. (*Exit.*)

THE DUCHESS OF MALFI (1614)

by John Webster

*DUKE FERDINAND is close to madness. He has long
had an obsessive relationship with his twin sister, the
eponymous Duchess, and on discovering that she has
contracted a secret marriage and borne two children,
has arranged for his mercenary, Bosola, to kill her. The
Duchess has just been strangled by Bosola.
FERDINAND arrives in her chamber to see the results
of his handiwork.*

Act IV, Scene II

FERDINAND: Cover her face; mine eyes dazzle: she
                                       died young.

[BOSOLA: I think not so; her infelicity
   Seem'd to have years too many.]

FERDINAND: She and I were twins;
   And should I die this instant, I had liv'd
   Her time to a minute.

[BOSOLA: It seems she was born first:
   You have bloodily approv'd the ancient truth,
   That kindred commonly do worse agree
   Than remote strangers.]

FERDINAND: Let me see her face
   Again. Why didst thou not pity her? What
   An excellent honest man mightst thou have been,
   If thou hadst borne her to some sanctuary!
   Or, bold in a good cause, oppos'd thyself,
   With thy advanced sword above thy head,

Between her innocence and my revenge!
I bade thee, when I was distracted of my wits,
Go kill my dearest friend, and thou has done't.
For let me but examine well the cause:
What was the meanness of her match to me?
Only I must confess I had a hope,
Had she continu'd widow, to have gain'd
An infinite mass of treasure by her death:
And that was the main cause, – her marriage,
That drew a stream of gall quite through my heart.
For thee, as we observe in tragedies
That a good actor many times is curs'd
For playing a villain's part, I hate thee for 't,
And, for my sake, say, thou has done much ill well.

[BOSOLA: Let me quicken your memory, for I perceive
You are falling into ingratitude: I challenge
The reward due to my service.]

FERDINAND: I'll tell thee
What I'll give thee.

[BOSOLA: Do.]

FERDINAND: I'll give thee a pardon
For this murder.

[BOSOLA: Ha!]

FERDINAND: Yes, and 'tis
The largest bounty I can study to do thee.
By what authority didst thou execute
This bloody sentence?

[BOSOLA: By yours.]

FERDINAND: Mine! Was I her judge?
Did any ceremonial form of law

Doom her to not-being? Did a complete jury
Deliver her conviction up i'the court?
Where shalt thou find this judgment register'd,
Unless in hell? See, like a bloody fool,
Thou'st forfeited thy life, and thou shalt die for 't.

THE PLAIN DEALER (1677)

by William Wycherley

This comedy concerns the cynical and misanthropic MANLY, a bluntly-spoken sea captain and adventurer. He has recently returned from the Dutch wars and no longer trusts anyone except his beloved Olivia, and his best friend, Vernish. In this speech, from the opening scene of the play, he explains to his friend, Freeman, how he has left his fortune in the hands of his beloved, Olivia. Unfortunately, he is shortly to discover that Olivia and Vernish have betrayed him.

Act I, Scene I

MANLY: She has Beauty enough to call in question her Wit or Virtue, and her Form wou'd make a starved Hermit, a Ravisher; yet her Virtue, and Conduct, wou'd preserve her from the subtil Lust of pamper'd Prelate. She is so perfect a Beauty, that Art cou'd not better it, nor Affectation deform it; yet all this is nothing. Her tongue as well as face, ne'r knew artifice; nor ever did her words or looks contradict her heart: She is all truth, and hates the lying, masking, daubing World, as I do; for which I love her, and for which I think she dislikes not me: for she has often shut out of her conversation for mine, the gaudy fluttering Parrots of the Town, Apes, and Echoes of men only, and refus'd their common place pert chat, flattery, and submissions, to be entertain'd with my sullen bluntness, and honest love. And, last of all, swore to me, since her Parents wou'd not suffer her to go with me, she wou'd stay behind for no other man; but follow me, without their leave, if not to be obtain'd. Which Oath – that she might the better keep it, I left her the value of five or six thousand pound: for Womens wants are generally their most importunate Solicitors to Love, or Marriage.

[FREEMAN: And Money summons Lovers, more than Beauty, and augments but their importunity, and their number; so makes it the harder for a Woman to deny 'em. For my part, I am for the *French* Maxim, if you wou'd have your Female Subjects Loyal, keep 'em poor: but, in short, that your Mistress may not marry, you have given her a Portion.]

MANLY: She had given me her heart first, and I am satisfi'd with the security; I can never doubt her truth and constancy.

[FREEMAN: It seems you do, since you are fain to bribe it with Money. But how come you to be so diffident of the Man that sayes he loves you, and not doubt the Woman that sayes it?]

MANLY: I shou'd (I confess) doubt the Love of any other Woman but her, as I do the friendship of any other Man but him I have trusted; but I have such proofs of their faith, as cannot deceive me.

[FREEMAN: Cannot!]

MANLY: Not but I know, that generally, no Man can be a great Enemy, but under the name of Friend; and if you are a Cuckold, it is your Friend only that makes you so; for your Enemy is not admitted to your house: if you are cheated in your Fortune, 'tis your Friend that does it; for your Enemy is not made your Trustee: if your Honour, or Good Name be injur'd, 'tis your

Friend that does it still, because your Enemy is not
believ'd against you. Therefore I rather choose to go
where honest, downright Barbarity is profest; where
men devour one another like generous hungry Lyons
and Tygers, not like Crocodiles; where they think the
Devil white, of our complexion, and I am already so
far an *Indian*: but, if your weak faith doubts this
miracle of a Woman, come along with me, and believe,
and thou wilt find her so handsom, that thou, who art
so much my Friend, wilt have a mind to lie with her,
and so will not fail to discover what her faith and thine
is to me.

THE ROVER (1677)

by Aphra Behn

The beautiful Angellica, a courtesan, has hung a picture outside her window, advertising her services for one thousand crowns per month. WILLMORE, a penniless but dashing Sea Captain newly landed in Naples, has seen the picture and is taken by her charms. He causes a scene with other suitors and follows Angellica into her house. She is utterly taken with him but pretends otherwise.

Act II, Scene II

WILLMORE: I am studying, Madam, how to purchase
  you, tho at present I am unprovided of Money.

[ANGELLICA: Sure, this from any other Man would
  anger me – nor shall he know the Conquest he has
  made – Poor angry Man, how I despise this railing.]

WILLMORE: Yes, I am poor – but I'm a Gentleman,
  And one that scorns this Baseness which you practice.
  Poor as I am, I would not sell myself,
  No, not to gain your charming high-priz'd Person.
  Tho I admire you strangely for your Beauty,
  Yet I contemn your Mind. –
  And yet I wou'd at any rate enjoy you;
  At your own rate – but cannot – See here
  The only Sum I can command on Earth;
  I know not where to eat when this is gone:
  Yet such a Slave I am to Love and Beauty,
  This last reserve I'll sacrifice to enjoy you. –
  Nay, do not frown, I know you are to be bought,

And wou'd be bought by me, by me,
For a mean trifling Sum, if I could pay it down.
Which happy knowledge I will still repeat,
And lay it to my Heart, it has a Virtue in't,
And soon will cure those Wounds your Eyes have made.–
And yet – there's something so divinely powerful there –
Nay, I will gaze – to let you see my Strength.

(*Holds her, looks on her, and pauses and sighs.*)

By Heaven, bright Creature – I would not for the
World
Thy Fame were half so fair as is thy Face.

(*Turns her away from him.*)

[ANGELLICA: (*Aside.*) His words go thro me to the
very Soul.

If you have nothing else to say to me.]

WILLMORE: Yes, you shall hear how infamous you are –
For which I do not hate thee:
But that secures my Heart, and all the Flames it feels
Are but so many Lusts,
I know it by their sudden bold intrusion.
The Fire's impatient and betrays, 'tis false –
For had it been the purer Flame of Love,
I should have pin'd and languish'd at your Feet,
E'er found the Impudence to have discover'd it.
I now dare stand your Scorn, and your Denial.

THE CITY HEIRESS (1682)

by Aphra Behn

In the years immediately after the Restoration of Charles II, Puritan feeling was still strong among members of the older generation. This has led Sir Timothy Treat-all to disapprove of the behaviour of his nephew and heir, the good-looking TOM WILDING, who has embraced the loose morals of London, ablaze with decadence after years of repression. Sir Timothy has threatened to cut TOM off without a penny by marrying again and having another heir. The young dandy is determined to live as he chooses, while thwarting his uncle's marital ambitions. Here, TOM is speaking to his friend, Sir Charles Meriwell, not knowing that the lady he is to meet in church, the Lady Galliard, is also the object of his friend's affections.

Act I

TOM WILDING: Well, dear Charles, let's sup together to night, and contrive some way to be reveng'd of this wicked uncle of mine. I must leave thee now, for I have an assignation here at church.

[SIR CHARLES MERIWELL: Hah! At Church!]

TOM WILDING: Ay, Charles, with the dearest She-Saint, and I hope sinner.

[SIR CHARLES MERIWELL: What, at Church? Pox, I shall be discover'd now in my Amours. That's an odd place for Love-Intrigues.]

TOM WILDING: Oh, I am to pass for a sober, discreet person to the relations; but for my mistress, she's made of no such sanctify'd materials; she is a widow, Charles, young, rich, and beautiful.

[SIR CHARLES MERIWELL: Hah! If this shou'd prove my Widow, now. (*Aside.*)]

TOM WILDING: And though at her own dispose, yet is much govern'd by honour, and a rigid mother, who is ever preaching to her against the vices of youth, and t'other end of the Town Sparks;[1] dreads nothing so much as her daughter's marrying a villainous Tory. So the young one is forc'd to dissemble religion, the best mask to hide a kind mistress in.

[SIR CHARLES MERIWELL: This must be my Lady Galliard. (*Aside.*)]

TOM WILDING: There is at present some ill understanding between us; some damn'd Honourable fop lays siege to her, which has made me ill received; and I having a new intrigue elsewhere, return her cold disdain, but now and then she crosses my heart too violently to resist her. In one of these hot fits I now am, and must find some occasion to speak to her.

[SIR CHARLES MERIWELL: By Heaven, it must be she – I am studying now, amongst all our She-Acquaintance, who this shou'd be.]

TOM WILDING: The dearest loveliest hypocrite, white as lilies, smooth as rushes, and plump as grapes after a shower, haughty her mein, her eyes full of disdain, and yet bewitching sweet; but when she loves soft, witty, wanton, all that charms a soul, and but for now and then a fit of honour, Oh, damn the nonsense! wou'd be all my own.

---

1 *town sparks* Fashionable young men about town

[SIR CHARLES MERIWELL: 'Tis she, By Heaven! (*Aside*.) Methinks this widow shou'd prove a good income to you, as things now stand between you and your uncle.]

TOM WILDING: Ah, Charles, but I am otherways dispos'd of. There is the most charming pretty thing in nature fallen in love with this person of mine, a rich City-Heiress, Charles, and I have her in possession.

[SIR CHARLES MERIWELL: How can you love two at once? I've been as wild and as extravagant, as youth and wealth cou'd render me; but ne'er arrived to that degree of lewdness, to deal my heart about: my hours I might, but love shou'd be entire.]

TOM WILDING: Ah, Charles, two such bewitching faces wou'd give thy heart the lie: – But love divides us, and I must into church. Adieu till night.

THE DOUBLE DEALER (1694)

by William Congreve

MELLEFONT is a personable young man in fashionable society, in love with and engaged to marry Cynthia, the daughter of Sir Paul and Lady Plyant. The wedding is due to take place tomorrow. However, his aunt, Lady Touchwood, has developed an all-consuming passion for MELLEFONT and is determined to break off his engagement. Here, at the Touchwood's house, MELLEFONT is speaking to his friend, Careless.

Act I, Scene III

MELLEFONT: I am jealous of a plot. I would have noise and impertinence keep my Lady Touchwood's head from working: for hell is not more busy than her brain, nor contains more devils than that imaginations.

[CARELESS: I thought your fear of her had been over. Is not to-morrow appointed for your marriage with Cynthia, and her father, Sir Paul Plyant, come to settle the writings this day on purpose?]

MELLEFONT: True; but you shall judge whether I have not reason to be alarmed. None besides you and Maskwell are acquainted with the secret of my Aunt Touchwood's violent passion for me. Since my first refusal of her addresses she has endeavoured to do me all ill offices with my uncle, yet has managed 'em with that subtlety, that to him they have borne the face of kindness; while her malice, like a dark lanthorn,[2] only shone upon me where it was directed. Still, it gave me less perplexity to prevent the success of her

2 *lanthorn* Lantern

displeasure than to avoid the importunities of her love, and of two evils I thought myself favoured in her aversion. But whether urged by her despair and the short prospect of time she saw to accomplish her designs; whether the hopes of revenge, or of her love, terminated in the view of this my marriage with Cynthia, I know not, but this morning she surprised me in my bed.

[CARELESS: Was there ever such a fury! 'Tis well nature has not put it into her sex's power to ravish. Well, bless us, proceed. What followed?]

MELLEFONT: What at first amazed me – for I looked to have seen her in all the transports of a slighted and revengeful woman – but when I expected thunder from her voice, and lightning in her eyes, I saw her melted into tears and hushed into a sigh. It was long before either of us spoke: passion had tied her tongue, and amazement mine. In short, the consequence was thus, she omitted nothing that the most violent love could urge, or tender words express; which when she saw had no effect, but still I pleaded honour and nearness of blood to my uncle, then came the storm I feared at first, for, starting from my bed-side like a fury, she flew to my sword, and with much ado I prevented her doing me or herself a mischief. Having disarmed her, in a gust of passion she left me, and in a resolution, confirmed by a thousand curses, not to close her eyes till they had seen my ruin.

[CARELESS: Exquisite woman! But what the devil, does she think thou hast no more sense than to get an heir upon her body to disinherit thyself? for as I take it this settlement upon you is, with a proviso, that your uncle have no children.]

MELLEFONT: Well, the service you are to do me will be
a pleasure to yourself: I must get you to engage my
Lady Plyant all this evening, that my pious aunt may
not work her to her interest. And if you chance to
secure her to yourself, you may incline her to mine.
She's handsome, and knows it; is very silly, and thinks
she has sense, and has an old fond husband.

THE WAY OF THE WORLD (1700)

by William Congreve

The plot of this satirical comedy is complex but the situation here is straightforward. MIRABEL is a handsome, wealthy and honourable young man of fashion, in love with the wayward, imperious and witty Millamant. In this famous scene, Millamant has just laid down the terms on which she will agree to be married. MIRABEL, with immense charm and courtesy, responds with his own terms. The couple adore each other and have been waiting for this moment for some time, each enjoying the chase. He uses a number of legal terms in making this contract.

Act IV, Scene V

MIRABEL: Your bill of fare is something advanced in this latter account. Well, have I liberty to offer conditions:– that when you are dwindled into a wife, I may not be beyond measure enlarged into a husband?

[MILLAMANT: You have free leave: propose your utmost, speak and spare not.]

MIRABEL: I thank you. *Imprimis*, then, I covenant that your acquaintance be general; that you admit no sworn confidant or intimate of your own sex; no she friend to screen her affairs under your countenance, and tempt you to make trial of a mutual secrecy. No decoy-duck to wheedle you a fop – scrambling to the play in a mask, then bring you home in a pretended fright, when you think you shall be found out, and rail at me for missing the play, and disappointing the frolic which you had to pick me up and prove my constancy.

[MILLAMANT: Detestable IMPRIMIS! I go to the play in a mask!]

MIRABEL: *Item*, I article, that you continue to like your own face as long as I shall, and while it passes current with me, that you endeavour not to new coin it. To which end, together with all vizards for the day, I prohibit all masks for the night, made of oiled skins and I know not what – hog's bones, hare's gall, pig water, and the marrow of a roasted cat. In short, I forbid all commerce with the gentlewomen in what-d'ye-call-it court. *Item*, I shut my doors against all bawds with baskets, and pennyworths of muslin, china, fans, atlases, etc. *Item,* when you shall be breeding –

[MILLAMANT: Ah, name it not!]

MIRABEL: Which may be presumed, with a blessing on our endeavours –

[MILLAMANT: Odious endeavours!]

MIRABEL: I denounce against all strait lacing, squeezing for a shape, till you mould my boy's head like a sugar-loaf, and instead of a man-child, make me father to a crooked billet. Lastly, to the dominion of the tea-table I submit; but with proviso, that you exceed not in your province, but restrain yourself to native and simple tea-table drinks, as tea, chocolate, and coffee. As likewise to genuine and authorised tea-table talk, such as mending of fashions, spoiling reputations, railing at absent friends, and so forth. But that on no account you encroach upon the men's prerogative, and presume to drink healths, or toast fellows; for prevention of which, I banish all foreign forces, all auxiliaries to the tea-table, as orange-brandy, all aniseed, cinnamon, citron, and Barbadoes waters, together with ratafia and the most noble spirit of clary. But for cowslip-wine, poppy-water, and all dormitives, those I allow. These provisos admitted, in other things I may prove a tractable and complying husband.

[MILLAMANT: Oh, horrid provisos! Filthy strong waters! I toast fellows, odious men! I hate your odious provisos.]

MIRABEL: Then we're agreed. Shall I kiss your hand upon the contract? And here comes one to be a witness to the sealing of the deed.

THE RECRUITING OFFICER (1706)

by George Farquhar

PLUME, the Recruiting Officer of the title, is in Lichfield to raise soldiers for the army. PLUME is a rakish fellow and is highly attracted to Silvia, daughter of the local Justice. Meeting his old friend, Worthy, PLUME explains his feelings about Silvia.

Act I, Scene I

PLUME: Your affairs had put mine quite out of my head. 'Tis true, Silvia and I had once agreed to go to bed together, could we have adjusted preliminaries; but she would have the wedding before consummation, and I was for consummation before the wedding – we could not agree. She was a pert obstinate fool, and would lose her maidenhead her own way, so she may keep it for Plume.

[WORTHY: But do you intend to marry upon no other conditions?]

PLUME: Your pardon, sir, I'll marry upon no condition at all, – if I should, I'm resolved never to bind myself to a woman for my whole life, till I know whether I shall like her company for half an hour. Suppose I married a woman that wanted a leg? Such a thing might be, unless I examined the goods beforehand. If people would but try one another's constitutions before they engaged, it would prevent all these elopements, divorces, and the devil knows what.

[WORTHY: Nay, for that matter, the town did not stick to say, that –]

PLUME: I hate country towns for that reason – if your town has a dishonourable thought of Silvia, it deserves to be burnt to the ground. – I love Silvia, I admire her frank, generous disposition; there's something in that girl more than woman, her sex is but a foil to her – the ingratitude, dissimulation, envy, pride, avarice, and vanity of her sister females, do but set off their contraries in her – in short, were I once a general, I would marry her.

DON JUAN (1736)

by Carlo Goldoni
Translated by Robert David MacDonald

PUBLISHED BY OBERON BOOKS (ISBN 1 870259 37 8)

The play is set in eighteenth-century Spain, where DON JUAN TENORIO, the legendary Neapolitan seducer of women, is an intelligent manipulator of every situation to his own advantage. In this speech he faces Don Alfonso, the prime minister to the King of Castile, to answer charges of seducing Donna Anna, daughter of a Castilian nobleman. DON JUAN's smooth tongue and well-marshalled arguments have a persuasive effect on Don Alfonso.

DON JUAN: I say, Señor, the face of Donna Anna
    blinded me – seduced me; I took fire
    at those fair eyes, and to the fire of love
    was added an indulgence, as unwise
    as it was liberal, in the pleasures of
    the table; an intemperance – unworthy
    of a noble soul! Oh, the unhappy chalice
    of two perfidious gods, Cupid and Bacchus!
    I blush to tell you; but I must not hide
    the truth from you, for, at that fatal moment,
    so utterly did desire supplant my reason,
    I was no longer master of myself.
    Ah, what unlucky star compelled my host
    to quit the table, leaving me alone
    and ardent at the side of so much beauty?
    My burning heart interpreted the event
    prompted by its desires: I boldly asked

the fair one for deliverance from my torment.
She answered with contemptuous modesty;
her rage lit up a further fire in me.
Reason by now had fled me; and my fury
carried me on to threats. At this sad juncture
her father entered, armed, deaf to excuses –
he challenged me. I, under provocation,
gave blow for blow, governed not by my will,
but by a cruel fate, which brought my sword
fatally to his breast. He fell, transfixed.
There, Señor, are my faults: I have confessed them.
Remember, though, that I was blindly led
by two blind, traitorous gods. If we could just
free from this stone the fallen hero's voice,
might it not plead for mercy for me now?
Perhaps he now repents not having curbed
his overpowering rage, perhaps he would
condone in me a wild excess of youth.
What use would my death be to him? What use
my blood to his reluctant, grieving daughter?
To remedy his injuries, he should ask
for something else from me, something whose justice
I hardly could deny, my hand in marriage
to her who, through my fault, is now in mourning.
If Don Juan dies will Donna Anna's honour
be thereby restored? Will she allow
the world to harbour doubts of whether she
defended her honour from a resolute lover
successfully, or did she fight in vain?
Poor Donna Anna! Overborne by grief,
she does not see the greatest of her dangers.
I go too far – I know. The criminal
cannot prescribe the punishment for his crime.
However, is it not legitimate

to ask for pity, just as it is to make
such sacrifice as will restore the damage
without the loss of blood? Ah, Don Alfonso,
speak you for me. You can obtain for me
the royal clemency, and Donna Anna
will be rewarded with my hand, while you,
though losing one friend, will have gained another,
less valorous, I grant, but no less faithful.
Be my protector. Not from love of life
am I urged now to ask your charity,
but love of blood, and care for reputation.
The mercy of the great King of Castile
is known to all the world, as is his justice.
May he not now give an example of it,
which will both profit him and do him honour?
It is not the punishment of a crime for which
the world reserves its wonder, but the clemency
of a merciful monarch, since the world is full
of wretched crimes, but poor in merciful kings.

FRIENDS AND LOVERS (1751)

by Carlo Goldoni
Translated by Robert David MacDonald

PUBLISHED BY OBERON BOOKS   (ISBN 1 870259 378)

Goldoni's comedy is set in Hamburg in the neighbouring apartments of Sebastian and Herr Mayer. The plot turns on misplaced and misunderstood letters, the resulting confusions spiralling into farce. FLORINDO has been staying with his friend, Sebastian. Sebastian is in love with his neighbour's daughter, Clara. FLORINDO has decided to leave Hamburg because he too has fallen in love with Clara. Little does he know that Sebastian's sister is carrying a torch for him.

Act I, Scene II

FLORINDO: I do not know where I am any longer. The conversation with Clara has utterly confused me. I did not ask to go there – Sebastian forced me. I think Clara realised I love her, just as I understood her to have an inclination for me. We parted somewhat unceremoniously. I feel obliged to see her again before I go, but if I go back there, it will be worse than ever.

[TRIVELLINO: (*Entering.*) Signore, a letter.

FLORINDO: Where from?

TRIVELLINO: I really couldn't say. From a woman, by the smell.]

FLORINDO: Here. Clara Mayer! From her! My heart beats.
'*Dearest Florindo...*' Dearest? To me, 'dearest'? The word brings me out in a cold sweat. '*Since you are*

determined on leaving...' Alas, I do not know how to resist. Discretion: let us not allow passion to veil our sight. Read it as an act of pure curiosity – civility. '*Since you are determined on leaving dearest Florindo...*' Oh, curse that 'dearest'. I read below, yet my eyes fly up to that. '*Since you are determined on leaving, and you do not, or pretend you do not know the state in which you leave me...*' Certainly I pretend, but, oh, I do know. '*I am constrained to open my heart to you.*' Do so, then, but I have made my decision. '*You must know, dearest Florindo...*' (Oh, that word again!) '*You must know...*' I can't see to read any more. '*You must know, dearest Florindo...*' Why cannot I just skip the word? '*Since I first saw you, I have been on fire...*' She has been on fire, and I have been burnt. '*...on fire with your deservings, and that without your presence near I shall most certainly expire...*' And so shall I; no matter if honour and friendship can be saved. '*Be moved to compassion, dearest friend.*' Again. The word tortures me, addressed to me by such a hand. I cannot go on. I cannot read it. Tear it up. Rid myself of it. What have I done? Tearing up a letter so full of kindness? Before finishing it? Not to know what she said at the end? If I could reassemble the pieces. '*Dearest Florindo...*' No!! No more! I will not torture myself any longer. But what am I thinking of? To leave without saying anything? It would be too cowardly, too indiscreet. I must reply. A few lines, well-considered. The matter is out, it is only fitting we speak clearly. To make her repent this love of hers, as I do mine. And if one day Sebastian should see my letter? Then he will see how I was capable of sacrificing my love, my heart, my life even. How can I begin? 'Dearest Clara...'? Hardly. If the word has the effect on her it had on me, she will die on the spot.

FRIENDS AND LOVERS (1751)

by Carlo Goldoni
Translated by Robert David MacDonald

PUBLISHED BY OBERON BOOKS (ISBN 1 870259 378)

*Goldoni's comedy is set in Hamburg in the neighbouring
apartments of Sebastian and HERR MAYER. The plot
turns on misplaced and misunderstood letters, the
resulting confusions spiralling into farce. HERR MAYER
is a comic elderly miser in the great tradition of Volpone
or Moliere's Harpagon. In this scene, we realise the
extent of his greed to vivid comic effect.*

Act II, Scene I

HERR MAYER: Nobody here to tease me. Don't want
the servants coming in on a pretext, of dusting or
sweeping. Bad enough they should have caught sight
of the big safe, where I keep the silver. I can't move
that; it's built into the wall. But after all, that's not
where I keep my best treasure, my great capital. (*He
takes out a strongbox.*) Here is my heart, my saint,
here is my redemption, my darling, my best beloved,
my gold. Oh, my dear, let me look at you. Let me
restore myself, console myself, feed myself with
gazing at you. My bread, my wine, my body, my life,
my precious viands, my pastime, my conversation: let
the idle go to the theatres, to parties, to balls. When I
see you, I dance, I rejoice. Gold, life of man, succour
of the poor, support of the great, triumph and calamity
of the human heart. Ah, every time I open you, my
heart pounds, for fear some alien rapacious hand has
violated you. Alas, my dear one, for three days now, I

have not added to you. Poor dear. Do not think I have left off loving you. I think of you waking, dream of you sleeping. To increase you, dear store, is all my care. I risk my money at twenty per cent; in less than ten years I shall give you a companion, no less strong, no less full than you. Ah, if I could live a thousand years, and every year bring you a new companion, and in the midst of a thousand chests, surrounded by you, my children, my children's children, to die… Die? Must I die? Poor chest. Must I leave you? Ah, I am in a sweat. Quickly, quickly, let me look at you again, my gold, my consolation. I cannot go on. Ah, fair coin of Portugal. How beautifully minted. I remember, I made you from all that grain I hoarded during the famine. All those unfortunates wailing because they had no bread, and there was I laughing, raking in the doubloons. And such beautiful gold marks, you could have been minted yesterday. I took you from that eldest son, who sold an estate on his father's death to pay me back 100 mark capital. What an affair.

SHE STOOPS TO CONQUER (1773)

by Oliver Goldsmith

A stormy night. TONY LUMPKIN, the loutish stepson of Mr Hardcastle, is involved in a plot to enable Hastings, an impoverished young man, to elope with Hardcastle's ward, Miss Neville. As well as getting the girl, Hastings must also get a diamond necklace which is her only inheritance – otherwise both will starve. TONY has inveigled the Hardcastles in a plot to get them out of the house and has had them driven around in circles in a carriage. Here he tells Hastings of the success of his plot.

Act V, Scene II

TONY: I'm your friend, and the best friend you have in the world, if you knew but all. This riding by night, by the bye, is cursedly tiresome. It has shook me worse than the basket of a stage-coach.

[HASTINGS: But how? where did you leave your fellow-travellers? Are they in safety? Are they housed?]

TONY: Five and twenty miles in two hours and a half is no such bad driving. The poor beasts have smoked for it: rabbit me, but I'd rather ride forty miles after a fox than ten with such varment.

[HASTINGS: Well, but where have you left the ladies? I die with impatience.]

TONY: Left them? Why where should I leave them but where I found them?

[HASTINGS: This is a riddle.]

TONY: Riddle me this then. What's that goes round the house, and round the house, and never touches the house?

[HASTINGS: I'm still astray.]

TONY: Why, that's it, mon. I have led them astray. By jingo, there's not a pond or a slough within five miles of the place but they can tell the taste of.

[HASTINGS: Ha! Ha! Ha! I understand: you took them in a round, while they supposed themselves going forward, and so you have at last brought them home again.]

TONY: You shall hear. I first took them down Feather-bed Lane, where we stuck fast in the mud. I then rattled them crack over the stones of Up-and-down Hill. I then introduced them to the gibbet on Heavy-tree Heath; and from that, with a circumbendibus, I fairly lodged them in the horse-pond at the bottom of the garden.

[HASTINGS: But no accident, I hope?]

TONY: No, no. Only mother is confoundedly frightened. She thinks herself forty miles off. She's sick of the journey; and the cattle can scarce crawl. So if your own horses be ready, you may whip off with cousin, and I'll be bound that no soul here can budge a foot to follow you.

[HASTINGS: My dear friend, how can I be grateful?]

TONY: Ay, now it's dear friend, noble 'squire. Just now, it was all idiot, cub, and run me through the guts. Damn your way of fighting, I say. After we take a knock in this part of the country, we kiss and be friends. But if you had run me through the guts, then I should be dead, and you might go kiss the hangman.

[HASTINGS: The rebuke is just. But I must hasten to relieve Miss Neville: if you keep the old lady employed, I promise to take care of the young one. (*Exit HASTINGS.*)]

TONY: Here she comes. Vanish. She's got from the pond, and draggled up to the waist like a mermaid.

THE RIVALS (1775)

by Richard Brinsley Sheridan

In Sheridan's romantic comedy, FAULKLAND is a young man deeply in love with Julia but cursed by a jealous nature. Everything she does or says causes him to doubt her, even though he loves her more than life. In this scene, he goes too far and causes her to break off their engagement. He is immediately remorseful.

Act III, Scene II

FAULKLAND: There now! so hasty, Julia! so anxious to be free! If your love for me were fixed and ardent, you would not lose your hold, even though I wished it!

[JULIA: Oh! you torture me to the heart! I cannot bear it.]

FAULKLAND: I do not mean to distress you. If I loved you less I should never give you an uneasy moment. But hear me. All my fretful doubts arise from this. Women are not used to weigh and separate the motives of their affections: the cold dictates of prudence, gratitude, or filial duty, may sometimes be mistaken for the pleadings of the heart. I would not boast – yet let me say, that I have neither age, person, nor character, to found dislike on; my fortune such as few ladies could be charged with indiscretion in the match. O Julia! when love receives such countenance from prudence, nice minds will be suspicious of its birth.

[JULIA: I know not whither your insinuations would tend:– but as they seem pressing to insult me, I will

spare you the regret of having done so. – I have given
you no cause for this! (*She exits in tears.*)]

FAULKLAND: In tears! Stay, Julia: stay but for a
moment – The door is fastened! – Julia! – my soul –
but for one moment! – I hear her sobbing! – 'Sdeath!
what a brute am I to use her thus! Yet stay! Ay – she
is coming now: – how little resolution there is in a
woman! – how a few soft words can turn them! – No,
faith! – she is not coming either. – Why, Julia – my
love – say but that you forgive me – come but to tell
me that – now this is being too resentful. Stay! she is
coming too – I thought she would – no steadiness in
anything: her going away must have been a mere trick
then – she shan't see that I was hurt by it. – I'll affect
indifference – (*Hums a tune; then listens.*) No –
zounds! she's not coming! – nor don't intend it, I
suppose. – This is not steadiness, but obstinacy! Yet I
deserve it. – What, after so long an absence to quarrel
with her tenderness! – 'twas barbarous and unmanly!
– I should be ashamed to see her now. – I'll wait till
her just resentment is abated – and when I distress her
so again, may I lose her for ever! and be linked instead
to some antique virago, whose gnawing passions, and
long hoarded spleen, shall make me curse my folly half
the day and all the night.

BRAND (1868)

by Henrik Ibsen
Translated and adapted by Robert David MacDonald

PUBLISHED BY OBERON BOOKS (ISBN 1 870259 27 0)

BRAND is a fiery priest-hero whose uncompromising belief in the ideal and his refusal to come to terms with mankind's flaws, brings tragedy and destruction. The play was originally written, in verse, to be read rather than performed, as it made technical demands which the theatre of the time could not meet. In this early scene, BRAND is walking the mountains in fog, with a walking staff and backpack. He has encountered some peasants who were afraid to travel with him for fear of an avalanche. BRAND has continued on alone.

BRAND: Dull slaves, creeping home. If you had
    lacked just the strength, but had the Will
    to strive, I would have helped you still,
    carried you with me, and been glad;
    breaking back and aching feet
    would just have made the journey sweet.
    But nobody can help the man
    who only wants the things he can.

    (*He goes on a little.*)

    Hm! Life, life – how it can be
    so dear to people puzzles me.
    Men will make every sacrifice
    but life. Then – not at any price!

    (*Smiles, as if at a memory.*)

I remember, when I was a boy,
two thoughts that caused me so much joy:
an owl scared of the dark, a fish
afraid of water. Though I'd wish
to think of something else – in vain:
those thoughts would fishhook in my brain.

Why? Why did they obsess my mind?
Because I, dimly, had divined
the gap between things as we see
them, and as they ought to be,
between the burdens which we must
endure, and those we call unjust.

And everybody, sick or whole,
is such a fish, or such an owl.
Born in darkness, he must work
down in the depths, live in the dark.
Yet it's just this makes him afraid:
splashing towards the shore, in dread,
he gazes on the stars at night,
and screams: Oh, give me air and light!

(*He pauses a moment, starts and listens.*)

What's that over there? It sounds like singing –
it is. I hear song mixed with ringing
laughter. The sun comes up, and through
the clearing mist I see a crowd
standing on the mountain side.
They're saying goodbye – most of them go
eastwards, but two have left the rest
and set their faces to the West.

(*The sun shines through the mist with increasing brightness. BRAND stands looking down at the two as they approach.*)

They wave goodbye. The glittering light
surrounds them both. The mist takes flight,
it seems, the hills are clothed with heather,
and heaven smiles on them together.
They must be siblings. Hand in hand,
they spring lightly across the heather:
The girl as weightless as a feather,
he slim and supple as a wand.

A WOMAN OF NO IMPORTANCE (1893)

by Oscar Wilde

GERALD ARBUTHNOT is an ambitious but badly-off young man who has been brought up carefully by his mother outside London. At a house party, GERALD meets and comes under the sway of the notorious Lord Illingworth, a fashionable and wealthy man about town. Illingworth offers GERALD a position as his secretary. What GERALD does not know, as he confronts his mother in this scene, is that Lord Illingworth is his father.

Act III

GERALD: Don't put it like that, mother. Of course I am sorry to leave you. Why, you are the best mother in the whole world. But after all, as Lord Illingworth says, it is impossible to live in such a place as Wrockley. You don't mind it. But I'm ambitious; I want something more than that. I want to have a career. I want to do something that will make you proud of me, and Lord Illingworth is going to help me. He is going to do everything for me.

[MRS ARBUTHNOT: Gerald, don't go away with Lord Illingworth. I implore you not to. Gerald, I beg you!]

GERALD: Mother, how changeable you are! You don't seem to know your own mind for a single moment. An hour and a half ago in the Drawing-room you agreed to the whole thing; now you turn round and make objections, and try to force me to give up my one chance in life. Yes, my one chance. You don't suppose that men like Lord Illingworth are to be found every day, do you, mother? It is very strange that when I have had such a wonderful piece of good luck, the one person to put difficulties in my way should be my own mother. Besides, you know, mother, I love Hester Worsley. Who could help loving her? I love her more than I have ever told you, far more. And if I had a position, if I had prospects, I could – I could ask her to – Don't you understand now, mother, what it means to me to be Lord Illingworth's secretary? To start like that is to find a career ready for one – before one – waiting for one. If I were Lord Illingworth's secretary I could ask Hester to be my wife. As a wretched bank clerk with a hundred a year it would be an impertinence.

[MRS ARBUTHNOT: I fear you need have no hopes of Miss Worsley. I know her views on life. She has just told them to me.]

(*A pause.*)

GERALD: Then I have my ambition left, at any rate. That is something – I am glad I have that! You have always tried to crush my ambition, mother – haven't you? You have told me that the world is a wicked place, that success is not worth having, that society is shallow, and all that sort of thing – well, I don't believe it, mother. I think the world must be delightful. I think society must be exquisite. I think success is a thing worth having. You have been wrong in all that you taught me, mother, quite wrong. Lord Illingworth is a successful man. He is a fashionable man. He is a man who lives in the world and for it. Well, I would give anything to be just like Lord Illingworth.

CANDIDA (1895)

by George Bernard Shaw

EUGENE MARCHBANKS is a doe-eyed, intense young man of 18 who believes himself to be a poet. MARCHBANKS has attached himself to the household of James Morell, a 'muscular Christian' preacher. In particular, MARCHBANKS has become romantically attached to Morell's wife, Candida, fifteen years his senior. He firmly believes his love is returned. MARCHBANKS' behaviour sets the cat among the pigeons in Morell's household. Here he is talking to Morell's secretary, Proserpine Garnett (Prossy), who is not sure how to handle him at all.

Act II

MARCHBANKS: Oh, then you are shy, like me. Isn't that so?

[PROSERPINE: Certainly I am not shy. What do you mean?]

MARCHBANKS: (*Secretly.*) You must be: that is the reason there are so few love affairs in the world. We all go about longing for love: it is the first need of our natures, the loudest cry of our hearts; but we dare not utter our longing: we are too shy. (*Very earnestly.*) Oh, Miss Garnett, what would you not give to be without fear, without shame –

[PROSERPINE: (*Scandalised.*) Well, upon my word!]

MARCHBANKS: (*With petulant impatience.*) Ah, don't say those stupid things to me: they don't deceive me:

what use are they? Why are you afraid to be your real self with me? I am just like you.

[PROSERPINE: Like me! Pray, are you flattering me or flattering yourself? I don't feel quite sure which. (*She turns to go back to the typewriter.*)]

MARCHBANKS: (*Stopping her mysteriously.*) Hush! I go about in search of love; and I find it in unmeasured stores in the bosoms of others. But when I try to ask for it, this horrible shyness strangles me; and I stand dumb, or worse than dumb, saying meaningless things – foolish lies. And I see the affection I am longing for given to dogs and cats and pet birds, because they come and ask for it. (*Almost whispering.*) It must be asked for: it is like a ghost: it cannot speak unless it is first spoken to. (*At his normal pitch, but with deep melancholy.*) All the love in the world is longing to speak; only it dare not, because it is shy, shy, shy. That is the world's tragedy. (*With a deep sigh he sits in the spare chair and buries his face in his hands.*)

[PROSERPINE: (*Amazed, but keeping her wits about her – her point of honor in encounters with strange young men.*) Wicked people get over that shyness occasionally, don't they?]

MARCHBANKS: (*Scrambling up almost fiercely.*) Wicked people means people who have no love: therefore they have no shame. They have the power to ask love because they don't need it: they have the power to offer it because they have none to give. (*He collapses into his seat, and adds, mournfully.*) But we, who have love, and long to mingle it with the love of others: we cannot utter a word. (*Timidly.*) You find that, don't you?

THE SEAGULL (1896)

by Anton Chekhov
Translated by Peter Gill

PUBLISHED BY OBERON BOOKS (ISBN 1 84002 150 0)

*KONSTANTIN is an intense and passionate young man.
His mother, Arkadina, is a celebrated actress who is not
happy about having a grown up son as it affects her
public image. KONSTANTIN has set up a stage beside
the lake on the family estate in order to produce an
experimental piece of drama which, he hopes, will prove
to his mother the integrity of his artistic ambitions. He is
talking to his uncle, Sorin.*

Act I

KONSTANTIN: (*Pulling petals off a flower.*) She loves
me. She loves me not. She loves me. She loves me
not. (*Laughing.*) You see, my mother does not love
me. No, she doesn't. As if I expected it. She wants to
live and love and wear clothes that are too young for
her and I'm 25 and a constant reminder that she is no
longer a girl. When I'm not there she's only 32. When
I am she's 43 and she hates me for that. She does.
She knows I don't believe in the theatre as she does.
She loves the theatre. She thinks she is serving
mankind and that it is a sacred art, while I think the
modern theatre is prescriptive, routine, conventional.
When the curtain goes up on the inevitable three-
walled room bright with artificial light, all these great
artists, these keepers of the sacred flame, all they do is
simply demonstrate how people eat, drink, make love,
move about, wear their jackets. And when from these

complacent *tableaux* with their meagre language they try to squeeze a moral, a mean, accessible little moral designed for domestic consumption, when in a thousand variations the same play is dished up over and over and over, I want to run away. Run away as Maupassant ran from the Eiffel Tower because it oppressed him with its vulgarity.

[SORIN: We couldn't do without the theatre.]

KONSTANTIN: We need new forms. New forms, and if we can't have them we'd better not have anything at all. (*Looking at his watch.*) I love my mother. I love her very much. But she leads such a silly life, carrying on with that novelist. Her name never out of the newspapers. I'm tired of it. The ordinary person in me is ashamed that my mother is an actress; I think if she was only like any other woman I might be happier.

Uncle, what a stupid, hopeless position I'm in. Sometimes she's at home to a houseful of famous people, writers, actors, and they only take any notice of me because I'm her son. Who am I? What am I? I left university in my third year owing to circumstances 'beyond our control'. I have no talent. I have no money. My passport says I'm an artisan from Kiev because my father was an artisan from Kiev before he became a famous actor. So when all these writers and actors in her drawing room condescend to notice me, I always think they're only measuring my insignificance. I guess what they think, and I suffer from the humiliation.

YOU NEVER CAN TELL (1897)

by George Bernard Shaw

*In this satirical comedy of manners, VALENTINE is a
pleasant, amusing young dentist in a seaside town on
the South Coast of England. He has two new clients –
Dolly and Philip Clandon – newly arrived from Madeira,
and is explaining the social mores of the town to them.
They have just invited him to lunch with them.*

Act I

VALENTINE: Now may I ask, to begin with, have you
ever been in an English seaside resort before? (*She
shakes her head slowly and solemnly. He turns to
Phil, who shakes his head quickly and
expressively.*) I thought so. Well, Mr Clandon, our
acquaintance has been short; but it has been voluble;
and I have gathered enough to convince me that you
are neither of you capable of conceiving what life in
an English seaside resort is. Believe me, it's not a
question of manners and appearance. In those
respects we enjoy a freedom unknown in Madeira.
(*Dolly shakes her head vehemently.*) Oh, yes, I
assure you. Lord de Cresci's sister bicycles in
knickerbockers; and the rector's wife advocates dress
reform and wears hygienic boots.

(*Dolly furtively looks at her own shoe. VALENTINE
catches her in the act, and deftly adds.*)

No, that's not the sort of boot I mean.

(*Dolly's shoe vanishes.*)

We don't bother much about dress and manners in England, because, as a nation we don't dress well and we've no manners. But – and now will you excuse my frankness?

(*They nod.*)

Thank you. Well, in a seaside resort there's one thing you must have before anybody can afford to be seen going about with you; and that's a father, alive or dead.

(*He looks at them alternately, with emphasis. They meet his gaze like martyrs.*)

Am I to infer that you have omitted that indispensable part of your social equipment?

(*They confirm him by melancholy nods.*)

Then I'm sorry to say that if you are going to stay here for any length of time, it will be impossible for me to accept your kind invitation to lunch.

(*He rises with an air of finality, and replaces the stool by the bench.*)

[PHILIP: (*Rising with grave politeness.*) Come, Dolly. (*He gives her his arm.*)

DOLLY: Good morning.

(*They go together to the door with perfect dignity.*)]

VALENTINE: (*Overwhelmed with remorse.*) Oh, stop, stop. (*They halt and turn, arm in arm.*) You make me feel a perfect beast.

[DOLLY: That's your conscience; not us.]

VALENTINE: (*Energetically, throwing off all pretence of a professional manner.*) My conscience! My conscience has been my ruin. Listen to me. Twice before I have set up as a respectable medical practitioner in various parts of England. On both occasions I acted conscientiously, and told my patients the brute truth instead of what they wanted to be told. Result, ruin. Now I've set up as a dentist, a five shilling dentist; and I've done with conscience forever. This is my last chance. I spent my last sovereign on moving in; and I haven't paid a shilling of rent yet. I'm eating and drinking on credit; my landlord is as rich as a Jew and as hard as nails; and I've made five shillings in six weeks. If I swerve by a hair's breadth from the straight line of the most rigid respectability, I'm done for. Under such a circumstance, is it fair to ask me to lunch with you when you don't know your own father?

[DOLLY: After all, our grandfather is a canon of Lincoln Cathedral.]

VALENTINE: (*Like a castaway mariner who sees a sail on the horizon.*) What! Have you a grandfather?

[DOLLY: Only one.]

VALENTINE: My dear, good young friends, why on earth didn't you tell me that before? A canon of Lincoln! That makes it all right, of course. Just excuse me while I change my coat.

THE MAN OF DESTINY (1897)

by George Bernard Shaw

This is a one-act play, rarely performed, and set in Northern Italy in 1796. NAPOLEON is a newly-promoted young general, here confronting a mysterious lady who has come to collect a secret dispatch from him.

NAPOLEON: (*Coming behind the couch.*) Tell me this. Suppose you could have got that letter by coming to me over the bridge at Lodi the day before yesterday! Suppose there had been no other way, and that this was a sure way – if only you escaped the cannon!

(*She shudders and covers her eyes for a moment with her hands.*)

Would you have been afraid?

[LADY: Oh, horribly afraid, agonizingly afraid. (*She presses her hands on her heart.*) It hurts only to imagine it.]

NAPOLEON: (*Inflexibly.*) Would you have come for the despatches?

[LADY: (*Overcome by the imagined horror.*) Don't ask me. I must have come.]

NAPOLEON: Why?

[LADY: Because I must. Because there would have been no other way.]

NAPOLEON: (*With conviction.*) Because you would have wanted my letter enough to bear your fear.

There is only one universal passion: fear. Of all the thousand qualities a man may have, the only one you will find as certainly in the youngest drummer boy in my army as in me, is fear. It is fear that makes men fight: it is indifference that makes them run away: fear is the mainspring of war. Fear! I know fear well, better than you, better than any woman. I once saw a regiment of good Swiss soldiers massacred by a mob in Paris because I was afraid to interfere: I felt myself a coward to the tips of my toes as I looked on at it. Seven months ago I revenged my shame by pounding that mob to death with cannon balls. Well, what of that? Has fear ever held a man back from anything he really wanted – or a woman either? Never. Come with me; and I will show you twenty thousand cowards who will risk death every day for the price of a glass of brandy. And do you think there are no women in the army, braver than the men, because their lives are worth less? Psha! I think nothing of your fear or your bravery. If you had had to come across to me at Lodi, you would not have been afraid: once on the bridge, every other feeling would have gone down before the necessity – the necessity – for making your way to my side and getting what you wanted. And now, suppose you had done all this – suppose you had come safely out with that letter in your hand, knowing that when the hour came, your fear had tightened, not your heart, but your grip of your own purpose – that it had ceased to be fear, and had become strength, penetration, vigilance, iron resolution – how would you answer then if you were asked whether you were a coward?

[LADY: (*Rising*.) Ah, you are a hero, a real hero.]

NAPOLEON: Pooh! There's no such thing as a real hero.

CAESAR AND CLEOPATRA (1901)

by George Bernard Shaw

Shaw's comedy tells the story of the relationship between kittenish young Cleopatra, Queen of Egypt, and ageing warrior Julius Caesar. His play begins with a long address to the audience by the Sphinx of Egypt. However, Shaw provided an alternative Prologue, from which this speech by the Egyptian warrior, BEL AFFRIS is taken. The Egyptians are bullish that they can defeat the invading Roman army but BEL AFFRIS, a brave and honourable man, is quick to explain exactly why Caesar's Romans are such a formidable enemy.

An Alternative Prologue

BEL AFFRIS: (*Stepping between them.*) Listen, cousin. Man to man, we Egyptians are as gods above the Romans.

[THE GUARDSMEN: (*Exultingly.*) Aha!]

BEL AFFRIS: But this Caesar does not pit man against man: he throws a legion at you where you are weakest as he throws a stone from a catapult; and that legion is as a man with one head, a thousand arms, and no religion. I have fought against them; and I know.

[BELZANOR: (*Derisively.*) Were you frightened, cousin? (*The guardsmen roar with laughter, their eyes sparkling at the wit of their captain.*)]

BEL AFFRIS: No, cousin; but I was beaten. They were frightened (perhaps); but they scattered us like chaff.

(The guardsmen, much dampened, utter a growl of contemptuous disgust.)

[BELZANOR: Could you not die?]

BEL AFFRIS: No: that was too easy to be worthy of a descendant of the gods. Besides, there was no time: all was over in a moment. The attack came just where we least expected it.

[BELZANOR: That shows that the Romans are cowards.]

BEL AFFRIS: They care nothing about cowardice, these Romans: they fight to win. The pride and honour of war are nothing to them.

[PERSIAN: Tell us the tale of the battle. What befell?

THE GUARDSMEN: *(Gathering eagerly around Bel Affris.)* Ay: the tale of the battle.]

BEL AFFRIS: Know then, that I am a novice in the guard of the temple of Ra in Memphis, serving neither Cleopatra nor her brother Ptolemy, but only the high gods. We went a journey to inquire of Ptolemy why he had driven Cleopatra into Syria, and how we of Egypt should deal with the Roman Pompey, newly come to our shores after his defeat by Caesar at Pharsalia. What, think ye, did we learn? Even that Caesar is coming also in hot pursuit of his foe, and that Ptolemy has slain Pompey, whose severed head he holds in readiness to present to the conqueror. *(Sensation among the guardsmen.)* Nay, more: we found that Caesar is already come; for we had not made half a day's journey on our way back when we came upon a city rabble flying from his legions, whose landing they had gone out to withstand.

[BELZANOR: And ye, the temple guard! Did you not withstand these legions?]

BEL AFFRIS: What man could, that we did. But there came the sound of a trumpet whose voice was as the cursing of a black mountain. Then saw we a moving wall of shields coming towards us. You know how the heart burns when you charge a fortified wall; but how if the fortified wall were to charge YOU?

[PERSIAN: (*Exulting in having told them so.*) Did I not say it?]

BEL AFFRIS: When the wall came nigh, it changed into a line of men – common fellows enough, with helmets, leather tunics, and breastplates. Every man of them flung his javelin: the one that came my way drove through my shield as through a papyrus – lo there! (*He points to the bandage on his left arm.*) and would have gone through my neck had I not stooped. They were charging at the double then, and were upon us with short swords almost as soon as their javelins. When a man is close to you with such a sword, you can do nothing with our weapons: they are all too long.

[PERSIAN: What did you do?]

BEL AFFRIS: Doubled my fist and smote my Roman on the sharpness of his jaw. He was but mortal after all: he lay down in a stupor; and I took his sword and laid it on. (*Drawing the sword.*) Lo! a Roman sword with Roman blood on it!

THE CHERRY ORCHARD (1904)

by Anton Chekhov
Translated by Peter Gill

PUBLISHED BY OBERON BOOKS (ISBN 1 870259 75 0)

The Ranevsky family can no longer afford to keep the family estate with its magnificent cherry orchard. The news that the land is to be sold off has a devastating effect on the family and the various dependent members of the household. Here TROFIMOV, a perpetual student, explains his vision of the future to Anya, the 17-year-old daughter of the family. TROFIMOV is an idealist and, like many of Chekhov's characters, his dreams are fragile.

TROFIMOV: The whole of Russia is our cherry orchard. This country is great and magnificent and full of the most wonderful places. (*A pause.*) Just think. Your family have been slave owners for generations. Your great-grandfather owned slaves and your grandfather owned slaves. They owned living souls. Do you see faces looking out of the cherry trees in the orchard? Can't you hear voices when the leaves move? They owned living souls. All of you, your whole family, from the first to the last, even you, Anya.

You none of you, not your mother nor your Uncle, nor even you, really know that you've incurred debt that you can never pay, that you're living at the expense of other people's happiness, of other people's lives – at the expense of people you won't let through the door. We're living out of our own time. We're living in the past – two hundred years in the past. We have no sense of history, because we have no history. We have no culture. We're stuck. So, we just philosophise and suffer from neurotic depression and drink vodka. But before we can begin to live in the present, we must find some way to expiate the past. To finish with it we must atone for it. And we shall only finish with it through suffering and by a great and ceaseless struggle. It's important that you understand this, Anya.

[ANYA: The house we live in hasn't been ours for a long time. I know that. I shall leave it, I promise you.

TROFIMOV: Yes leave it. And if you have any keys to it, throw them into a well. Be like the wind – free!

ANYA: (*Rapturously*.) Yes I will. You speak so beautifully, Pyetia!]

TROFIMOV: You must believe what I say, Anya. You must. I'm not thirty yet and I know I'm still a student but I've suffered a great deal. I may be young but I've experienced more than you can imagine. Every winter I get ill and hungry and anxious. I live like a beggar all winter long and there's hardly anything I haven't experienced. That's been my destiny. And yet I can never give up. Every moment of the day and night my soul is filled with hope and a vision of the future. I sense great happiness, Anya. I can see it coming…

BLOOD WEDDING (1933)

by Federico Garcia Lorca
Translated by Gwynne Edwards

PUBLISHED BY METHUEN (ISBN 0 413 15780 6)

This brief, poetic and bloody tragedy explores the profound and direct passions of Spanish peasant life. On her wedding day, a bride jilts her groom and runs off with her former lover, Leonardo. The bridegroom pursues them into the forest, determined to get his revenge. Above the forest rises the MOON, whom Lorca personifies as a young woodcutter with a white face. The stage takes on a strange blue light as he enters and makes the following speech.

Act III, Scene I

MOON: Round swan on the river,
    Eye of the cathedrals,
    False dawn amongst the leaves
    Am I; they shall not escape!
    Who is hiding? Who is sobbing
    In the thick brush of the valley?
    The moon places a knife
    Abandoned in the sky,
    That is a leaden ambush
    And longs to be the pain of blood.
    Let me come in! I come frozen
    From walls and windows!
    Open up roofs and hearts
    Where I can warm myself!
    I am cold! My ashes
    Of dreaming metal

Seek the crest of fire
Through mountains and through streets.
But the snow bears me
On its back of jasper,
And water drowns me
Cold and hard in pools.
And so tonight there'll be
Red blood to fill my cheeks,
And the rushes forming clusters
At the wide feet of the wind.
Let there be no shadow, no hidden corner
To which they can escape!
For I want to enter a breast
Where I can warm myself!
A heart for me!
Warm!, that will spill
Over the mountains of my breast;
Let me come in, oh, let me in!
(*To the branches*.) I don't want shadows. My rays
Must enter everywhere,
And let there be among dark trunks
A murmur of gleaming light,
So that tonight there'll be
Red blood to fill my cheeks,
And the rushes forming clusters
At the wide feet of the wind.
Who is hiding? Come out, I say!
No! They shan't get away!
For I shall make the horse shine
With fever bright as diamond.

II: FEMALE MONOLOGUES

ANTIGONE (442 BC)

by Sophocles
English version by Declan Donnellan

PUBLISHED BY OBERON BOOKS (ISBN 1 84002 136 5)

The two sons of the banished King Oedipus led a failed rebellion against Creon, King of Thebes, and both were killed. Creon ordered that their bodies remain unburied but ANTIGONE, the sister of the dead men, insisted on burying them. In defying Creon, ANTIGONE is condemned to death by immolation. This is her last speech before being entombed alive.

ANTIGONE: I move now to my tomb, my bridal bed.
 I go to see my family again,
 My own people. So many of them dead,
 It's time to turn the key and shove the door.
 They're getting ready on the other side.
 The doorway is most terrible for me.
 I go last and far too young but I hope
 You'll kiss me soon father, mother, brother.
 You must, Polynices, since I washed you,
 Adorned you and poured libations on your grave
 And this is my reward for loving you.
 Some people, decent people, brave people
 Think that I did right. I tell you frankly,
 Never would I do this for a husband;
 Nor would I dare this, even for my child.
 Only for you, Polynices… Why so?
 My husband could die and I could marry,
 My child could die, my womb could bear another
 But Oedipus and Jocasta cannot

Make another brother for Antigone.
This is why I did you special honour.
He thought that what I did to you was wrong.
Oh my poor brother! You're here; you're so pale.
That's it! Take my hands! No, there is no bed.
No wedding song is sung. No child will cry.
Which of the Gods' laws does he say I broke?
And why should I expect the Gods to help?
Will none of you help me? I did my best
And so I was condemned. Do the Gods smile?
I forgive them for all my sufferings.
But if it is these men who do the wrong,
Then, then, may they suffer no more than this.

MEDEA (431 BC)

by Euripides
Translated by Alistair Elliot

PUBLISHED BY OBERON BOOKS (ISBN 1 870259 36 X)

MEDEA helped the hero Jason to defeat her father, the King of Colchis, so Jason married her and she bore him two children. Returned to his home town of Thebes, Jason finds himself a hero and is offered the hand in marriage of the King's daughter. To make this possible, he must divorce and abandon MEDEA, who will be banished from Thebes. MEDEA reacts violently to this news. Here, when Jason has come to 'reason with her', she gives him short shrift.

MEDEA: You come to us, where you're most hated, here?
    Is this your courage and heroic boldness,
    To wrong your friends, then look them in the face?
    No: it's that worst disease of human minds,
    A blank where shame should be. But I am glad you came:
    It makes my heart a little easier
    To spear you with my words, and watch you writhe.

    I'll begin at the beginning.
    I saved your life, as every Greek can witness
    Who joined you in the voyage of the Argo;
    (I helped you catch the fire-breathing oxen
    And harness them, and sow the fatal field;)
    I killed the dragon, the sleepless sentinel
    That wound its coils around the Golden Fleece;
    I held the light of safety over you.
    I chose to desert my father and my home
    To come with you to Iolcos: full of love,

Empty of thought, in those days. After that, I killed
King Pelias, using his own daughters' hands
For the unkindest death, to wipe his blood-line out.
I did all that for you, and now you drop me;
You take a new wife, seeming to forget
That we have children. If you were a childless man,
One might forgive your lusting for her bed...
But all your oaths and promises are broken:
I cannot trust you now. Nor can I understand
What you believe in – do you think the gods
That used to govern us no longer do?
You seem to imagine the moral law has changed –
But even you must realise you've not kept your word.
Look at this hand you took in yours so often,
These knees you clung to, begging me to help:
The meaningless embraces of a bad
Husband! The hopes I entertained and lost!

Come on! I shall confide in you, like some old friend –
There's nothing I can gain from you, I know that,
But still – I can expose your shame with questions:
Where can I turn to, now? Home to my father?
I betrayed my home and country to come with you.
To the grieving daughters of King Pelias?
A fine welcome they'd give me
      In the house where I killed their father.
It comes to this: the friends I had at home
Now hate me; and in other places too
Where I need not have harmed a soul, I did,
Because you asked me to. They hate me now as well.
So in return for that, you made me 'happy' –
Greek women think so, anyway: 'What a wonderful
And faithful man that lucky woman has!'
This husband who calmly lets me go, to exile,

Without a friend, alone with fatherless children –
A fine beginning for a newly-married man,
That his children and the woman who saved his life
Must wander abroad in cringing beggary.

Oh Zeus, why did you give humanity
The clearest evidence when gold is false –
But set no markings on the skin of man
To single out the bad one from the good?

AJAX (c 410 BC)

by Sophocles
Translated by James Kerr

PUBLISHED BY OBERON BOOKS (ISBN 1 84002 105 5)

Ajax is the King of Salamis and, after Achilles, the bravest of the key figures in the Greek camp laying siege to Troy. After the death of Achilles, Ajax and Odysseus fight for the dead hero's weapons. When they are allotted to Odysseus, Ajax goes mad with rage. In this scene, his loyal wife TECMESSA tells the Chorus about her husband's strange behaviour and her fears for his future.

TECMESSA: I know
    In the middle of the night when all the campfires were out
    He picked up his sword and walked towards the door
                        of our hut
    He said nothing to me, so I asked him what he was doing
    You see I had to ask, there was no messenger calling him
    And I know that there was no trumpet so I asked him
                    what he was doing
    'Everyone's asleep…my love, where are you going'
    He turned to me and his words were cold
    'Woman, silence makes a woman beautiful'
    That was all
    He left
    I didn't follow
    So, you see, I don't know what he did out there
    But he did return, bringing beasts
    He'd beaten them
    I watched him chop off heads

I watched him hang some up by their feet
I watched him slit throats open, and slice down spines
He said he'd taught them such a lesson
He checked outside, scattered unholy words to the night
I could hear his laughter, I could hear his pride
Then, in one moment (It was as if he was thrown)
He fell at my feet and stopped
And born slowly back into his senses
In pain
He shook
His troubled soul rudely woken
Sitting in the bloody ruin
Bodies and Silence
Trembling flesh
He bruised his head with his fists
And scratched the hair from his own head
(…In blood…)
He cried
But there were no words
We sat and I did nothing
Finally he did speak to me
Threats
He said he would hurt me if I didn't tell him every
                                        detail
Everything that had happened
Friends, I was afraid so I told him all I have told you
He let out another cry
But this was a sound I had never heard from him
                                        before
(He used to laugh at the weakness of simple tears
When he was sad he was my groaning bull)
But now he's broken
I've tried food and drink
He won't

He sits, silent
Among his beasts
I can see that his mind is thinking something
Planning something
That's why I came out to you
Help him, please
Friends
Please go in and try to help him

HENRY VI PART 1 (c 1592)

by William Shakespeare

*England and France have been at war for years. A young
woman, JOAN LA PUCELLE (known to history as Joan
of Arc) claims to have heard voices from God telling her
to lead the French armies. She goes to the court to meet
the Dauphin, Charles, whom she plans to make a
legitimate King of France. In order to test her miraculous
powers, Charles hides at the back of the group, inviting
Reignier to impersonate him. JOAN sees through his trick.
Though modern sensibilities see JOAN as a saint, to
Shakespeare and his contemporaries she was a witch,
in league with the devil.*

Act I, Scene II

JOAN: Reignier, is't thou that thinkest to beguile me?
   Where is the Dauphin? Come, come from behind;
   I know thee well, though never seen before.
   Be not amaz'd, there's nothing hid from me:
   In private will I talk with thee apart.
   Stand back, you lords, and give us leave a while.

[REIG: She takes upon her bravely at first dash.]

JOAN: Dauphin, I am by birth a shepherd's daughter,
   My wit untrain'd in any kind of art.
   Heaven and our Lady gracious hath it pleas'd
   To shine on my contemptible estate:
   Lo! whilst I waited on my tender lambs,
   And to sun's parching heat display'd my cheeks,
   God's mother deigned to appear to me,
   And in a vision full of majesty

Will'd me to leave my base vocation
And free my country from calamity:
Her aid she promis'd and assur'd success;
In complete glory she reveal'd herself;
And, whereas I was black and swart before,
With those clear rays which she infus'd on me,
That beauty am I bless'd with which you see.
Ask me what question thou canst possible
And I will answer unpremeditated:
My courage try by combat, if thou dar'st,
And thou shalt find that I exceed my sex.
Resolve on this, thou shalt be fortunate
If thou receive me for thy war-like mate.

[CHAR: Thou hast astonish'd me with thy high terms.
    Only this proof I'll of thy valour make,
    In single combat thou shalt buckle with me,
    And if thou vanquishest, thy words are true;
    Otherwise I renounce all confidence.]

JOAN: I am prepar'd: here is my keen-edg'd sword,
    Deck'd with five flower-de-luces on each side;
    The which at Touraine, in Saint Katharine's
                                    churchyard,
    Out of a great deal of old iron I chose forth.

[CHAR: Then come, o' God's name; I fear no woman.]

JOAN: And, while I live, I'll ne'er fly from a man.

ALL'S WELL THAT ENDS WELL (c 1604)

by William Shakespeare

HELENA, daughter of a distinguished physician and ward of the Countess of Rousillon, is in love with the Countess's son, Bertram. Bertram does not return her affection. When Bertram goes to the court of the King of France, who is sick, HELENA follows. Using skills her father taught her, she cures the King. When offered a reward of her choice, she asks for Bertram's hand in marriage. The King grants her request but Bertram flees before the marriage can be consummated, leaving behind a letter. This speech is HELENA's response to that letter.

Act III, Scene II

HELENA: 'Till I have no wife, I have nothing in France.'
    Nothing in France until he has no wife!
    Thou shalt have none, Rousillon, none in France;
    Then hast thou all again. Poor lord! is't I
    That chase thee from thy country and expose
    Those tender limbs of thine to the event
    Of the non-sparing war? and is it I
    That drive thee from the sportive court, where thou
    Wast shot at with fair eyes, to be the mark
    Of smoky muskets? O you leaden messengers,
    That ride upon the violent speed of fire,
    Fly with false aim; move the still-piecing air,
    That sings with piercing; do not touch my lord.
    Whoever shoots at him, I set him there;
    Whoever charges on his forward breast,
    I am the caitiff that do hold him to't;

And, though I kill him not, I am the cause
His death was so effected: better 'twere
I met the ravin lion when he roar'd
With sharp constraint of hunger; better 'twere
That all the miseries which nature owes
Were mine at once. No, come thou home, Rousillon,
Whence honour but of danger wins a scar,
As oft it loses all: I will be gone;
My being here it is that holds thee hence:
Shall I stay here to do't? no, no, although
The air of paradise did fan the house
And angels officed all: I will be gone,
That pitiful rumour may report my flight,
To consolate thine ear. Come, night; end, day!
For with the dark, poor thief, I'll steal away.

THE WHITE DEVIL (1608)

by John Webster

This violent tragedy, based on fact, tells the story of VITTORIA COROMBONA, who becomes the mistress of the Duke of Brachiano. Having seduced her and implicated her in the murder of his Duchess, Brachiano turns against VITTORIA, believing malicious gossip about her. Here she protests to Brachiano at his treatment of her and demonstrates the spirit which made her so attractive to him in the first place.

Act IV, Scene II

VITTORIA: I'll live so now I'll make that world recant
   And change her speeches. You did name your Duchess.

[BRACHIANO: Whose death God pardon.]

VITTORIA: Whose death God revenge
   On thee most godless Duke.

[FLAMINEO: Now for two whirlwinds.]

VITTORIA: What have I gain'd by thee but infamy?
   Thou hast stain'd the spotless honour of my house,
   And frighted thence noble society:
   Like those, which sick o'th' palsy, and retain
   Ill-scenting foxes 'bout them, are still shunn'd
   By those of choicer nostrils. What do you call this house?
   Is this your palace? Did not the judge style it
   A house of penitent whores? Who sent me to it?
   Who hath the honour to advance Vittoria
   To this incontinent college? Is't not you?
   Is't not your high preferment? Go, go brag

How many ladies you have undone, like me.
Fare you well sir; let me hear no more of you.
I had a limb corrupted to an ulcer,
But I have cut it off: and now I'll go
Weeping to heaven on crutches. For your gifts,
I will return them all; and I do wish
That I could make you full executor
To all my sins. O that I could toss myself
Into a grave as quickly: for all thou art worth
I'll not shed one tear more; – I'll burst first.

(*She throws herself upon a bed.*)

THE PLAIN DEALER (1676)

by William Wycherley

*Manly, a bluntly-spoken sea captain and adventurer has
returned from the Dutch wars to discover that his beloved
OLIVIA has betrayed him, appropriated his fortune and
married his best friend, Vernish. She is now unfaithful
even to Vernish. Fidelia, a young woman who has
followed Manly to sea dressed in men's clothing, offers
to intercede with OLIVIA, and visits her in her lodgings
at night. OLIVIA believes herself to be receiving a lover.*

Act V, Scene III

OLIVIA: So, are you there?

(*Enter Fidelia, followed softly by Manly.*)

Come, my dear punctual Lover, there is not such
another in the World; thou hast Beauty and Youth to
please a Wife; Address and Wit, to amuse and fool a
Husband; nay, thou hast all things to be wish'd in a
Lover, but your Fits: I hope, my Dear, you won't have
one to night; and, that you may not, I'll lock the door,
tho' there be no need of it, but to lock out your Fits;
for my Husband is just gone out of Town again. Come,
where are you?

(*Goes to the door and locks it.*)

[MANLY: Well, thou hast impudence enough to give me
    Fits too, and make Revenge it self impotent, hinder me
    from making thee yet more infamous, if it can be.]

OLIVIA: Come, come, my Soul, come.

[FIDELIA: Presently, my Dear: we have time enough
    sure.]

OLIVIA: How! time enough! True Lovers can no more
    think they ever have time enough, than love enough:
    You shall stay with me all night; but that is but a
    Lover's moment. Come.

[FIDELIA: But won't you let me give you and my self
    the satisfaction of telling you, how I abus'd your
    Husband last night?]

OLIVIA: Not when you can give me, and your self too,
    the satisfaction of abusing him again, to night. Come.

[FIDELIA: Let me but tell you how your Husband –]

OLIVIA: O name not his, or Manly's more loathsom
    name, if you love me; I forbid 'em last night: and you
    know I mention'd my Husband but once, and he came.
    No talking pray; 'twas ominous to us. You make me
    fancy a noise at the door already, but I'm resolv'd not
    to be interrupted.

(*A noise at the door.*)

Where are you? Come; for, rather than lose my dear
expectation now, tho' my Husband were at the door,
and the bloody Ruffian Manly here in the room, with
all his awful insolence, I wou'd give my self to this
dear hand, to be led away, to Heavens of joys, which
none but thou canst give. But, what's this noise at the
door? So, I told you what talking wou'd come to.

(*The noise at the door increases.*)

Ha! – O Heavens, my Husbands voice! –

(*OLIVIA listens at the door.*)

[MANLY: Freeman is come too soon. (*Aside*.)]

OLIVIA: O 'tis he! – Then here is the happiest minute
lost, that ever bashful Boy, or trifling Woman fool'd
away! I'm undone! my Husbands reconcilement too
was false, as my joy, all delusion: but, come this way,
here's a Back-door.

THE OLD BACHELOR (1693)

by William Congreve

The Prologues and Epilogues to Restoration plays, addressed by the actor directly to the audience, are often extremely pointed and witty pieces in their own right. This Prologue, with its conceit of a young actress forgetting her lines, was originally spoken by Mrs Bracegirdle, a popular comedienne of her day.

The Prologue

How this vile world is changed! In former days
Prologues were serious speeches before plays,
Grave, solemn things, as graces are to feasts,
Where poets begged a blessing from their guests.
But now no more like suppliants we come;
A play makes war, and prologue is the drum.
Armed with keen satire and with pointed wit,
We threaten you who do for judges sit,
To save our plays, or else we'll damn your pit.
But for your comfort, it falls out to-day,
We've a young author and his first-born play;
So, standing only on his good behaviour,
He's very civil, and entreats your favour.
Not but the man has malice, would he show it,
But on my conscience he's a bashful poet;
You think that strange – no matter, he'll outgrow it.
Well, I'm his advocate: by me he prays you
(I don't know whether I shall speak to please you),
He prays – O bless me! what shall I do now?
Hang me if I know what he prays, or how!
And 'twas the prettiest prologue as he wrote it!

Well, the deuce take me, if I han't forgot it.
O Lord, for heav'n's sake excuse the play,
Because, you know, if it be damned to-day,
I shall be hanged for wanting what to say.
For my sake then – but I'm in such confusion,
I cannot stay to hear your resolution.

(*Runs off.*)

LOVE FOR LOVE (1695)

by William Congreve

ANGELICA is a lively and wilful young woman of fortune who is in love with Valentine, a young nobleman much troubled by debts. ANGELICA has to use all her manipulative skills to ensure they end up together. In this scene, ANGELICA is talking to her uncle, Foresight, and her Nurse. Foresight is a superstitious old fool who claims to be an astrologer.

Act II, Scene II

ANGELICA: But my inclinations are in force; I have a mind to go abroad, and if you won't lend me your coach, I'll take a hackney or a chair, and leave you to erect a scheme, and find who's in conjunction with your wife. Why don't you keep her at home, if you're jealous of her when she's abroad? You know my aunt is a little retrograde (as you call it) in her nature. Uncle, I'm afraid you are not lord of the ascendant, ha, ha, ha!

[FORESIGHT: Well, Jill-flirt, you are very pert, and always ridiculing that celestial science.]

ANGELICA: Nay, uncle, don't be angry – if you are, I'll reap up all your false prophecies, ridiculous dreams, and idle divinations. I'll swear you are a nuisance to the neighbourhood. What a bustle did you keep against the last invisible eclipse, laying in provision as 'twere for a siege. What a world of fire and candle, matches and tinder-boxes did you purchase! One would have thought we were ever after to live under ground, or at least making a voyage to Greenland, to inhabit there all the dark season.

[FORESIGHT: Why, you malapert slut –]

ANGELICA: Will you lend me your coach, or I'll go on – nay, I'll declare how you prophesied popery was coming only because the butler had mislaid some of the apostle spoons, and thought they were lost. Away went religion and spoon-meat together. Indeed, uncle, I'll indite you for a wizard.

[FORESIGHT: How, hussy! Was there ever such a provoking minx?

NURSE: O merciful father, how she talks!]

ANGELICA: Yes, I can make oath of your unlawful midnight practices, you and the old nurse there –

[NURSE: Marry, heaven defend! I at midnight practices? O Lord, what's here to do? I in unlawful doings with my master's worship – why, did you ever hear the like now? Sir, did ever I do anything of your midnight concerns but warm your bed, and tuck you up, and set the candle and your tobacco-box and your urinal by you, and now and then rub the soles of your feet? O Lord, I!]

ANGELICA: Yes, I saw you together through the key-hole of the closet one night, like Saul and the witch of Endor, turning the sieve and shears, and pricking your thumbs, to write poor innocent servants' names in blood, about a little nutmeg grater which she had forgot in the caudle-cup. Nay, I know something worse, if I would speak of it.

[FORESIGHT: I defy you, hussy; but I'll remember this, I'll be revenged on you, cockatrice. I'll hamper you. You have your fortune in your own hands, but I'll find a way to make your lover, your prodigal spendthrift gallant, Valentine, pay for all, I will.]

ANGELICA: Will you? I care not, but all shall out then. Look to it, nurse: I can bring witness that you have a great unnatural teat under your left arm, and he another; and that you suckle a young devil in the shape of a tabby-cat, by turns, I can.

[NURSE: A teat, a teat – I an unnatural teat! Oh, the false, slanderous thing; feel, feel here, if I have anything but like another Christian. (*Crying*.)

FORESIGHT: I will have patience, since it is the will of the stars I should be thus tormented. This is the effect of the malicious conjunctions and oppositions in the third house of my nativity; there the curse of kindred was foretold. But I will have my doors locked up; – I'll punish you: not a man shall enter my house.]

ANGELICA: Do, uncle, lock 'em up quickly before my aunt come home. You'll have a letter for alimony to-morrow morning. But let me be gone first, and then let no mankind come near the house, but converse with spirits and the celestial signs, the bull and the ram and the goat. Bless me! There are a great many horned beasts among the twelve signs, uncle. But cuckolds go to heaven.

THE WAY OF THE WORLD (1700)

by William Congreve

The wayward, imperious and witty MILLAMANT, a young lady of fortune, is in love with Mirabel, a handsome, wealthy and honourable young man of fashion. In this famous scene, MILLAMANT lays down the terms on which she will agree to be married. The couple adore each other and have been waiting for this moment for some time, each enjoying the chase.

Act IV, Scene V

MILLAMANT: Oh, I hate a lover that can dare to think he draws a moment's air independent on the bounty of his mistress. There is not so impudent a thing in nature as the saucy look of an assured man confident of success: the pedantic arrogance of a very husband has not so pragmatical an air. Ah, I'll never marry, unless I am first made sure of my will and pleasure.

[MIRABEL: Would you have 'em both before marriage? Or will you be contented with the first now, and stay for the other till after grace?]

MILLAMANT: Ah, don't be impertinent. My dear liberty, shall I leave thee? My faithful solitude, my darling contemplation, must I bid you then adieu? Ay-h, adieu. My morning thoughts, agreeable wakings, indolent slumbers, all ye *douceurs,* ye *sommeils du matin,* adieu. I can't do't, 'tis more than impossible – positively, Mirabel, I'll lie a-bed in a morning as long as I please.

[MIRABEL: Then I'll get up in a morning as early as I
    please.]

MILLAMANT: Ah! Idle creature, get up when you will.
    And d'ye hear, I won't be called names after I'm
    married; positively I won't be called names.

[MIRABEL: Names?]

MILLAMANT: Ay, as wife, spouse, my dear, joy, jewel,
    love, sweet-heart, and the rest of that nauseous cant,
    in which men and their wives are so fulsomely familiar
    – I shall never bear that. Good Mirabel, don't let us be
    familiar or fond, nor kiss before folks, like my Lady
    Fadler and Sir Francis; nor go to Hyde Park together
    the first Sunday in a new chariot, to provoke eyes and
    whispers, and then never be seen there together again,
    as if we were proud of one another the first week, and
    ashamed of one another ever after. Let us never visit
    together, nor go to a play together, but let us be very
    strange and well-bred. Let us be as strange as if we
    had been married a great while, and as well-bred as if
    we were not married at all.

[MIRABEL: Have you any more conditions to offer?
    Hitherto your demands are pretty reasonable.]

MILLAMANT: Trifles; as liberty to pay and receive visits
    to and from whom I please; to write and receive
    letters, without interrogatories or wry faces on your
    part; to wear what I please, and choose conversation
    with regard only to my own taste; to have no obligation
    upon me to converse with wits that I don't like,
    because they are your acquaintance, or to be intimate
    with fools, because they may be your relations. Come
    to dinner when I please, dine in my dressing-room

when I'm out of humour, without giving a reason. To have my closet inviolate; to be sole empress of my tea-table, which you must never presume to approach without first asking leave. And lastly, wherever I am, you shall always knock at the door before you come in. These articles subscribed, if I continue to endure you a little longer, I may by degrees dwindle into a wife.

DON JUAN (1736)

by Carlo Goldoni
Translated by Robert David MacDonald
PUBLISHED BY OBERON BOOKS (ISBN 1 870259 37 8)

*The play is set in eighteenth century Spain. Don Juan
Tenorio, the legendary Neapolitan seducer of women,
once made DONNA ISABELLA fall in love with him and
then abandoned her. She has followed him to Spain and
is currently disguised as a man. Here she confronts her
seducer and reveals her true identity.*

DONNA ISABELLA: Caballero,
    slacken your pace; I have to speak with you.

[DON JUAN: I do not know you, sir, another time…]

DONNA ISABELLA: Don Juan! Have you effaced my
    image from your memory, as well as from your heart?
    Can you not see in me the unhappy woman,
    deluded and deceived by you, who has
    disguised herself to follow you? You monster!
    How can you pretend you do not know me?

[DON JUAN: You say you are a woman? Dressed as a man?
    And that I am the man who has betrayed you,
    who promised to be true to you, and failed?
    I do not recall.]

DONNA ISABELLA: Not recall Isabella?
    The grief that frets my pride, the tears, the sighs,
    the vigils, and the hardships of my journey,
    perhaps all these have altered my appearance;
    my name alone, though, should beget remorse

and shame in you: shake off your lethargy,
recall the oaths you made to Heaven, to God.

[DON JUAN: I have no recollection of such oaths.]

DONNA ISABELLA: Did you not swear fidelity to me,
did you not swear love?

[DON JUAN: I only know
I have never sworn to keep faith with a woman.]

DONNA ISABELLA: I understand. You wish to say, you liar,
you infidel, that if you called me wife,
you said it with your lips and not your heart;
that you pretended love to me, and now
my trust, too great, has lost me my rash love;
now you deride me, and despise my grief.
My faith dishonoured, that is not a dream.
My love despised, no, nor is that a dream.
Betrayer, it is useless to pretend
not to recall my face, my name, our love.
Traitor, to hide is useless; for I know you
all too well; if you refuse to give me
justice for the love you have betrayed,
I shall exact revenge on you in blood.
Draw your sword! Now let me lose my life
along with yours, or recompense my injuries!

[DON JUAN: Friend, I am not accustomed to pay heed
to lunatics. To draw my sword against you
would be the basest cowardice.]

DONNA ISABELLA: Whether or not
I am a lunatic, the trial of arms will tell.
You had the courage to abandon me;
would you be less bold now in killing me?
What am I saying? You are the one to die.

FRIENDS AND LOVERS (1751)

by Carlo Goldoni
Translated by Robert David MacDonald

PUBLISHED BY OBERON BOOKS (ISBN 1 870259 37 8)

The plot of Goldoni's comedy turns on misplaced and misunderstood letters, the resulting confusions spiralling into farce. The play is set in Hamburg in the neighbouring apartments of Sebastian and Herr Mayer. Florindo has been staying with his friend, Sebastian. Sebastian is in love with his neighbour's daughter, Clara. Florindo has decided to leave Hamburg because he too has fallen in love with Clara. Little does Florindo know that Sebastian's sister STELLA has fallen in love with him and, in this scene, discovers a half-finished letter intended for Clara which she persuades herself is in fact for her.

Act I, Scene III

STELLA: (*Entering.*) Florindo still does not show his face. Can he be indifferent to my love? Yet I have seen him look at me with some attention. Has he no opinion of me? Yet he has addressed some kind words to me. Yes, and been happy to joke with me often enough, and now he behaves harshly, like this, to me? Is he to leave tomorrow? In my despite? What shall I do? The mere thought makes me shudder. What is this? Florindo's writing. '*Signora…*' Oh, heavens, who is he writing to? It is not finished. Jealousy consumes me. '*Unfortunately, I have inferred that you have a kindness for me. It is for this reason I have resolved to leave sooner than I intended,*

*since, finding your own inclination similar to my
own, I would no longer be able to behave towards
you with indifference.'* Could this be addressed to
me? Could he be in love with me, as I with him? No,
what obstacle could there be to his unburdening his
love and enjoying mine? This is to some other woman.
How can I get at the mystery? *'My friend Sebastian
has received me in his house, shared with me all
the secrets of his heart. What would he say of me,
were I to betray my friendship and hospitality?'*
Oh, heavens, it is me he is speaking of, he thinks if he
took advantage of Sebastian's trust to lay siege to his
sister's heart…no, my dearest, it is no bad action to
love those who love you. No love is reprehensible that
can end in a marriage to the liking of the friend
himself. I see now why you refuse to have relations
with me, you are afraid of displeasing my brother,
'betraying his hospitality'. *'You yourself feel it is not
fitting that…'* There the letter ends: but there my
hopes begin. 'Not fitting…' But it *is* fitting to speak in
good time, to reveal the secret, and mutually console
our loving hearts. Here is my brother, most apropos.
What? has some accident occurred?

(*Sebastian enters, his head bandaged.*)

THE HOUSEKEEPER (1758)

by Carlo Goldoni
Translated by Robert David MacDonald

PUBLISHED BY OBERON BOOKS (ISBN 1 870259 48 3)

*GIUSEPPINA and her sister Rosina are in high dudgeon.
They live with their uncle and they believe his
housekeeper, Valentina, has set out to snare him into
marriage. Forceful, snobbish and spirited GIUSEPPINA
is determined to prevent the alliance and, in this scene,
explains her plan to Rosina.*

Act III

GIUSEPPINA: Sister, let us have one thing clear. That
insolent woman is too overbold to be borne; and our
uncle, blind to her malice, does us an injustice for the
sake of a servant.

[ROSINA: Really it is a thing one cannot suffer; nobody I
talk to can understand. But I have worked out what's
going on. Sister, Valentina has bewitched our uncle.]

GIUSEPPINA: Bewitched fiddlesticks! I pique myself on
being an observer of such things; I know the whole
run of her enchantment. Listen, sister, that woman
came to this house as a kitchen-maid, oh-so-demure to
begin with; standing, eyes downcast, not saying a
peep. If she chanced to hear a licentious word, she put
her face in her apron, making out to be shocked. She
performed her duties with keenness and care, put
herself to work in the master's quarters: every second,
she would appear in front of him with work in her
hands. She heard his orders without looking him in the
face; if he made a joke, she would smile; when he

went out, she'd help him on with his coat, and help him off with it when he came back. Every morning, when he was barely awake, there she was at his bedside with his chocolate; every evening, she'd put him in his dressing-gown, and tell him the day's happenings in the neighbourhood. To stay at his side, she had the patience to play *tresette* with him for a penny a point. A little flattery, a little gossip and a deal of dedication, sufficed to make him fall in love with her. And once she had succeeded in that, she formed the design of becoming the mistress here. Getting bolder by the day, she set the other servants at variance, egging them on, uncovering various disagreements in the family: cunningly mixing truth and lies, she started setting us against each other. Thinking her a woman of judgment, the old man took her from the kitchen, and made her housekeeper. Now she commands in this house more than the master of it: from what he says, he wants to marry her. And the only witchcraft needed for a common slut of a servant to arrive at that is simple female cunning.

[ROSINA: Sister, you know so much about it all, I should have thought you capable of doing just as much.]

GIUSEPPINA: I am not capable of using similar wiles, but I know about them, and it will be enough to repair their damage. I have told our aunt Dorotea about it all: she will be here shortly, and be privy to our plan. As our mother's sister, she has every right to defend us against our inhuman uncle.

[ROSINA: But she is such a hothead, she will start with an uproar, and be at screaming pitch by tonight. Seriously, sister, if she does not moderate her vice this time, it could be a disaster.]

GUISEPPINA: Let be what will be, it has to finish one day.

THE RIVALS (1775)

by Richard Brinsley Sheridan

In Sheridan's romantic comedy, LYDIA LANGUISH is a romantic and very rich young woman. Her aunt wishes her to marry Captain Absolute but she has fallen in love with a penniless young ensign, Beverley – only to discover that Beverley is none other than Captain Absolute in disguise. Though delighted to be betrothed to the man she loves, she is rather sore about being tricked and regrets the loss of her 'romantic' young ensign. She is talking to her cousin, Julia.

Act V, Scene I

LYDIA: Heigh-ho! Though he has used me so, this fellow runs strangely in my head. I believe one lecture from my grave cousin will make me recall him.

(*Re-enter Julia.*)

O Julia, I have come to you with such an appetite for consolation. – Lud! child, what's the matter with you? You have been crying! – I'll be hanged if that Faulkland has not been tormenting you.

[JULIA: You mistake the cause of my uneasiness! – Something has flurried me a little. Nothing that you can guess at. – (*Aside.*) I would not accuse Faulkland to a sister!]

LYDIA: Ah! whatever vexations you may have, I can assure you mine surpass them. You know who Beverley proves to be?

[JULIA: I will now own to you, Lydia, that Mr Faulkland had before informed me of the whole affair. Had young Absolute been the person you took him for, I should not have accepted your confidence on the subject, without a serious endeavour to counteract your caprice.]

LYDIA: So, then, I see I have been deceived by every one! But I don't care – I'll never have him.

[JULIA: Nay, Lydia]

LYDIA: Why, is it not provoking? when I thought we were coming to the prettiest distress imaginable, to find myself made a mere Smithfield bargain of at last! There, had I projected one of the most sentimental elopements! – so becoming a disguise! – so amiable a ladder of ropes! – Conscious moon – four horses – Scotch parson – with such surprise to Mrs Malaprop – and such paragraphs in the newspapers! – Oh, I shall die with disappointment!

[JULIA: I don't wonder at it!]

LYDIA: Now – sad reverse! – what have I to expect, but, after a deal of flimsy preparation, with a bishop's license, and my aunt's blessing, to go simpering up to the altar; or perhaps be cried three times in a country church, and have an unmannerly fat clerk ask the consent of every butcher in the parish to join John Absolute and Lydia Languish, spinster! Oh that I should live to hear myself called spinster!

[JULIA: Melancholy, indeed!]

LYDIA: How mortifying, to remember the dear delicious shifts I used to be put to, to gain half a minute's conversation with this fellow! How often have I stole forth, in the coldest night in January, and found him in the garden, stuck like a dripping statue! There would he kneel to me in the snow, and sneeze and cough so pathetically! he shivering with cold and I with apprehension! and while the freezing blast numbed our joints, how warmly would he press me to pity his flame, and glow with mutual ardour! – Ah, Julia, that was something like being in love.

THE RIVALS (1775)

by Richard Brinsley Sheridan

In Sheridan's romantic comedy, Faulkland is a young man deeply in love with JULIA but cursed by a jealous nature. Everything she does or says causes him to doubt her. She has had enough. Faulkland has just given her a 'love test' too many and, though he confesses to it, JULIA can bear no more of his constant doubts.

Act V, Scene I

JULIA: Hold, Faulkland! – that you are free from a crime, which I before feared to name, Heaven knows how sincerely I rejoice! These are tears of thankfulness for that! But that your cruel doubts should have urged you to an imposition that has wrung my heart, gives me now a pang more keen than I can express.

[FAULKLAND: By Heavens! Julia –]

JULIA: Yet hear me, – My father loved you, Faulkland! and you preserved the life that tender parent gave me; in his presence I pledged my hand – joyfully pledged it – where before I had given my heart. When, soon after, I lost that parent, it seemed to me that Providence had, in Faulkland, shown me whither to transfer without a pause, my grateful duty, as well as my affection; hence I have been content to bear from you what pride and delicacy would have forbid me from another. I will not upbraid you, by repeating how you have trifled with my sincerity.

[FAULKLAND: I confess it all! yet hear –]

JULIA: After such a year of trial, I might have flattered myself that I should not have been insulted with a new probation of my sincerity, as cruel as unnecessary! I now see it is not in your nature to be content or confident in love. With this conviction – I never will be yours. While I had hopes that my persevering attention, and unreproaching kindness, might in time reform your temper, I should have been happy to have gained a dearer influence over you; but I will not furnish you with a licensed power to keep alive an incorrigible fault, at the expense of one who never would contend with you.

[FAULKLAND: Nay, but, Julia, by my soul and honour, if after this –]

JULIA: But one word more. – As my faith has once been given to you, I never will barter it with another. – I shall pray for your happiness with the truest sincerity; and the dearest blessing I can ask of Heaven to send you will be to charm you from that unhappy temper, which alone has prevented the performance of our solemn engagement. All I request of you is, that you will yourself reflect upon this infirmity, and when you number up the many true delights it has deprived you of, let it not be your least regret, that it lost you the love of one who would have followed you in beggary through the world!

(*She exits.*)

BRAND (1868)

by Henrik Ibsen
Translated and adapted by Robert David MacDonald

PUBLISHED BY OBERON BOOKS (ISBN 1 870259 27 0)

*Brand is a fiery priest-hero whose uncompromising belief
in the ideal and his refusal to come to terms with
mankind's flaws, brings tragedy and destruction. The
play was originally written, in verse, to be read rather
than performed as it made technical demands which the
theatre of the time could not meet. AGNES has fallen in
love with Brand's idealism and married him, but it proves
unhappy. They have a child, who dies. Brand can offer
AGNES no comfort, concentrating only on his plan to
build his church. AGNES starts to disintegrate psycho-
logically.*

Act IV

(*He goes into his room.*)

AGNES: Shut! Everything is shut! Shut off –
    even oblivion is denied me.
    Tears are forbidden, sighs cut off
    while they lie half-formed inside me.
    I must go out: I can't breathe the air
    in these lonely rooms. But where?
    Where is 'out?' Unrelenting eyes
    gaze down at me from lowering skies.
    Must I leave my heart's ease here?
    Can I fly from my silent fear?

(*She listens for a moment at BRAND's door.*)

Reading aloud: he cannot hear.
No help or comfort anywhere.
At Christmas God has too much to do
with the rich and happy, to listen to
a lonely mother's tale of woe.

(*Cautiously going over to the window.*)

If I did draw the shutters back,
the light would shine out through the crack,
and chase night's terrors from his black
sleeping-place. But no, he's not there.
Christmas is the children's time:
perhaps he'll be allowed to come;
perhaps he is already here!
Wasn't that a child's voice?
Ulf, I don't know what to do!
Your father has shut up the house.
I dare not open it for you.
You're an obedient little boy,
we never did anything to annoy him.
Fly home to Heaven – go back! fly!
Just don't let them see you cry.
Don't tell them your father locked
you out, when you came and knocked.
It's hard for a little boy like you
to know what grown-ups must go through.
Tell them he sorrows, say he grieves,
tell them how he picked the leaves
to weave into the wreath, how he
made it for you. Look! Can you see?

(*Listens, starts and shakes her head.*)

I'm dreaming! There's so much to be done
before we meet again, my son.

I must work, silently, to fulfil
his every demand. I'll steel
myself, stiffen up my will.
But tonight is Christmas, though
different from a year ago.
But shh! it is a holy night;

I shall take my treasures out,
relics saved from the shipwreck of
my happiness, impossible
to value, and accessible
only to a mother's love.

(*She kneels in front of a chest, opens a drawer and
removes various articles. At the same moment Brand
opens his door, and is about to say something to her,
when he sees what she is doing, and stands there
silent, and unnoticed by her.*)

Here are his christening robe and shawl.
And here's his smock – dear God! How sweet
and pretty. How smart he looked in it,
sitting up in church. And all
his other things, his scarf, the coat
he wore when it was freezing out;
the first time that he put it on,
it was too long – but not for long.
Here are the things I wrapped him in
for making the long journey South…
After I'd put them back again,
I was so tired – tired to death.

[BRAND: (*Wringing his hands.*)
    Spare me, Lord! Must I shatter these
    last lingering idolatries?
    Send another hand than mine.]

AGNES: It feels wet – have I been crying?
   Oh, still to possess this treasure
   makes me rich beyond all measure.

A DOLL'S HOUSE (1879)

by Henrik Ibsen
Translated by Michael Meyer

PUBLISHED BY METHUEN (ISBN 0 413 46340 0)

NORA HELMER is a young wife married to a successful banker. The mother of three small children, her husband's attitudes keep her very much a girl-wife, or a 'doll'. However, unknown to Helmer, NORA has helped him out of a difficult financial situation by forging her father's signature on a legal document. In this scene she is reunited with her childhood friend, Christine Linde, and is explaining how clever she has been.

Act I

NORA: He's so proud of being a man – it'd be so painful and humiliating for him to know that he owed anything to me. It'd completely wreck our relationship. This life we have built together would no longer exist.

[MRS LINDE: Will you never tell him?]

NORA: (*Thoughtfully, half-smiling.*) Yes – some time, perhaps. Years from now, when I'm no longer pretty. You mustn't laugh! I mean, of course, when Torvald no longer loves me as he does now; when it no longer amuses him to see me dance and dress up and play the fool for him. Then it might be useful to have something up my sleeve. (*Breaks off.*) Stupid, stupid, stupid! That time will never come. Well, what do you think of my big secret, Christine? I'm not completely useless, am I? Mind you, all this has caused me a frightful lot of worry. It hasn't been easy for me to

meet my obligations punctually. In case you don't
know, in the world of business there are things called
quarterly instalments and interest, and they're a
terrible problem to cope with. So I've had to scrape a
little here and save a little there, as best I can. I
haven't been able to save much on the housekeeping
money, because Torvald likes to live well; and I
couldn't let the children go short of clothes – I couldn't
take anything out of what he gives me for them. The
poor little angels!

[MRS LINDE: So you've had to stint yourself, my poor
Nora?]

NORA: Of course. Well, after all, it was my problem.
Whenever Torvald gave me money to buy myself new
clothes, I never used more than half of it; and I always
bought what was cheapest and plainest. Thank heaven
anything suits me, so that Torvald's never noticed. But
it made me a bit sad sometimes, because it's lovely to
wear pretty clothes. Don't you think?

[MRS LINDE: Indeed it is.]

NORA: And then I've found one or two other sources of
income. Last winter I managed to get a lot of copying
to do. So I shut myself away and wrote every evening,
late into the night. Oh, I often got so tired, so tired. But
it was great fun, though, sitting there working and
earning money. It was almost like being a man.

[MRS LINDE: But how much have you managed to pay
off like this?]

NORA: Well, I can't say exactly. It's awfully difficult to
keep an exact check on these kind of transactions. I
only know I've paid everything I've managed to

scrape together. Sometimes I really didn't know where to turn. (*Smiles.*) Then I'd sit here and imagine some rich old gentleman had fallen in love with me –

[MRS LINDE: What! What gentleman?]

NORA: Silly! And that now he'd died and when they opened his will it said in big letters: 'Everything I possess is to be paid forthwith to my beloved Mrs Nora Helmer in cash.'

[MRS LINDE: But, Nora dear, who was this gentleman?]

NORA: Great heavens, don't you understand? There wasn't any old gentleman; he was just something I used to dream up as I sat here evening after evening wondering how on earth I could raise some money. But what does it matter? The old bore can stay imaginary as far as I'm concerned, because now I don't have to worry any longer! (*Jumps up.*) Oh, Christine, isn't it wonderful? I don't have to worry any more! No more troubles! I can play all day with the children, I can fill the house with pretty things, just the way Torvald likes. And, Christine, it'll soon be spring, and the air'll be fresh and the skies blue – and then perhaps we'll be able to take a little trip somewhere. I shall be able to see the sea again. Oh, yes, yes, it's a wonderful thing to be alive and happy!

MRS WARREN'S PROFESSION (1888)

by George Bernard Shaw

Vivie Warren is an intelligent and independent young woman who has just graduated from Cambridge. She has been brought up apart from her mother, MRS WARREN, a widow who lives in Europe. In fact, MRS WARREN began life as a prostitute and has made her fortune from running a series of brothels in Europe. Here she explains her decision to Vivie.

Act II

MRS WARREN: What is any respectable girl brought up to do but to catch some rich man's fancy and get the benefit of his money by marrying him? – as if a marriage ceremony could make any difference in the right or wrong of the thing! Oh, the hypocrisy of the world makes me sick! Liz and I had to work and save and calculate just like other people; elseways we should be as poor as any good-for-nothing drunken waster of a woman that thinks her luck will last for ever. (*With great energy.*) I despise such people: theyve no character; and if theres a thing I hate in a woman, it's want of character.

[VIVIE: Come now, mother: frankly! Isn't it part of what you call character in a woman that she should greatly dislike such a way of making money?]

MRS WARREN: Why, of course. Everybody dislikes having to work and make money; but they have to do it all the same. I'm sure Ive often pitied a poor girl, tired out and in low spirits, having to try to please some man that she doesnt care two straws for – some half-drunken fool that thinks he's making himself agreeable when he's teasing and worrying and disgusting a woman so that hardly any money could pay her for putting up with it. But she has to bear with disagreeables and take the rough with the smooth, just like a nurse in a hospital or anyone else. It's not work that any woman would do for pleasure, goodness knows; though to hear the pious people talk you would suppose it was a bed of roses.

[VIVIE: Still, you consider it worth while. It pays.]

MRS WARREN: Of course it's worth while to a poor girl, if she can resist temptation and is good-looking and well conducted and sensible. It's far better than any other employment open to her. I always thought that it oughtnt to be. It cant be right, Vivie, that there shouldnt be better opportunities for women. I stick to that: it's wrong. But it's so, right or wrong; and a girl must make the best of it. But of course it's not worth while for a lady. If you took to it youd be a fool; but I should have been a fool if I'd taken to anything else.

SALOMÉ (1892)

by Oscar Wilde

Wilde's one act play is based on the Biblical story of Salomé, the niece of King Herod who demanded the head of John the Baptist in return for dancing for her uncle. The play was banned in Britain during Wilde's lifetime. It was originally written in French and translated by Wilde's lover, Lord Alfred Douglas. SALOMÉ has conceived a passion for John the Baptist (Jokanaan) who rejects her advances. In this scene, she attempts to seduce the chained Jokanaan.

SALOMÉ: Jokanaan, I am amorous of thy body! Thy body is white like the lilies of a field that the mower hath never mowed. Thy body is white like the snows that lie on the mountains, like the snows that lie on the mountains of Judæa, and come down into the valleys. The roses in the garden of the Queen of Arabia are not so white as thy body. Neither the roses in the garden of the Queen of Arabia, nor the feet of the dawn when they light on the leaves, nor the breast of the moon when she lies on the breast of the sea… There is nothing in the world so white as thy body. Let me touch thy body.

[JOKANAAN: Back! Daughter of Babylon! By woman came evil into the world. Speak not to me. I will not listen to thee. I listen but to the voice of the Lord God.]

SALOMÉ: Thy body is hideous. It is like the body of a leper. It is like a plastered wall where vipers have

crawled; like a plastered wall where the scorpions
have made their nest. It is like a whitened sepulchre
full of loathsome things. It is horrible, thy body is
horrible. It is of thy hair that I am enamoured,
Jokanaan. Thy hair is like clusters of grapes, like the
clusters of black grapes that hang from the vine-trees
of Edom in the land of the Edomites. Thy hair is like
the cedars of Lebanon, like the great cedars of
Lebanon that give their shade to the lions and to the
robbers who would hide themselves by day. The long
black nights, when the moon hides her face, when the
stars are afraid, are not so black. The silence that
dwells in the forest is not so black. There is nothing in
the world so black as thy hair... Let me touch thy hair.

[JOKANAAN: Back, daughter of Sodom! Touch me not.
Profane not the temple of the Lord God.]

SALOMÉ: Thy hair is horrible. It is covered with mire
and dust. It is like a crown of thorns which they have
placed on thy forehead. It is like a knot of black
serpents writhing round thy neck. I love not thy hair...
It is thy mouth that I desire, Jokanaan. Thy mouth is
like a band of scarlet on a tower of ivory. It is like a
pomegranate cut with a knife of ivory. The
pomegranate-flowers that blossom in the garden of
Tyre, and are redder than roses, are not so red. The
red blasts of trumpets, that herald the approach of
kings, and make afraid the enemy, are not so red. Thy
mouth is redder than the feet of those who tread the
wine in the wine-press. Thy mouth is redder than the
feet of the doves who haunt the temples and are fed
by the priests. It is redder than the feet of him who
cometh from a forest where he hath slain a lion, and
seen gilded tigers. Thy mouth is like a branch of coral

that fishers have found in the twilight of the sea, the coral that they keep for the kings…! It is like the vermilion that the Moabites find in the mines of Moab, the vermilion that the kings take from them. It is like the bow of the King of the Persians, that is painted with vermilion, and is tipped with coral. There is nothing in the world so red as thy mouth… Let me kiss thy mouth.

LADY WINDERMERE'S FAN (1892)

by Oscar Wilde

LADY WINDERMERE is a young wife who is distressed when Mrs Erlynne enters her husband's life. Mrs Erlynne is a woman with a scandalous past who is, unknown to her, LADY WINDERMERE's mother. LADY WINDERMERE believes her husband to be scandalously involved with Mrs Erlynne. She has written Windermere a letter and taken refuge in the rooms of Lord Darlington. If she is discovered there, she will be disgraced. Alone, she considers her position.

Act III

LADY WINDERMERE: Why doesn't he come? This waiting is horrible. He should be here. Why is he not here, to wake by passionate words some fire within me? I am cold – cold as a loveless thing. Arthur must have read my letter by this time. If he cared for me, he would have come after me, would have taken me back by force. But he doesn't care. He's entrammelled by this woman – fascinated by her – dominated by her. If a woman wants to hold a man, she has merely to appeal to what is worst in him. We make gods of men and they leave us. Others make brutes of them and they fawn and are faithful. How hideous life is!… Oh! it was mad of me to come here, horribly mad. And yet, which is the worst, I wonder, to be at the mercy of a man who loves one, or the wife of a man who in one's own house dishonours one? What woman knows? What woman in the whole world? But will he love me always, this man to whom

I am giving my life? What do I bring him? Lips that have lost the note of joy, eyes that are blinded by tears, chill hands and icy heart. I bring him nothing. I must go back – no; I can't go back, my letter has put me in their power – Arthur would not take me back! That fatal letter! No! Lord Darlington leaves England to-morrow. I will go with him – I have no choice.

(*Sits down for a few moments. Then starts up and puts on her cloak.*)

No, no! I will go back, let Arthur do with me what he pleases. I can't wait here. It has been madness my coming. I must go at once. As for Lord Darlington – Oh! here he is! What shall I do? What can I say to him? Will he let me go away at all? I have heard that men are brutal, horrible… Oh!

(*Hides her face in her hands.*)

LADY WINDERMERE'S FAN (1892)

by Oscar Wilde

Wilde could never resist creating portraits of society matrons. The DUCHESS OF BERWICK (who could be of any age from mid-thirties upwards) is one of his most appealing creations, a woman who believes herself good natured and supportive but who is ruled by protocol, gossip and malice. Here she can hardly wait to break the news to Lady Windermere of her husband's mysterious and scandalous behaviour.

Act I

DUCHESS OF BERWICK: Agatha, darling!

[LADY AGATHA: Yes, mamma.]

DUCHESS OF BERWICK: Will you go out on the terrace and look at the sunset?

[LADY AGATHA: Yes mamma. (*Exit through window, left.*)]

DUCHESS OF BERWICK: Sweet girl! So devoted to sunsets! Shows such refinement of feeling, does it not? After all, there is nothing like Nature, is there?

[LADY WINDERMERE: But what is it, Duchess? Why do you talk to me about this person?]

DUCHESS OF BERWICK: Don't you really know? I assure you we're all so distressed about it. Only last night at dear Lady Jansen's every one was saying how extraordinary it was that, of all men in London, Windermere should behave in such a way.

[LADY WINDERMERE: My husband – what has HE
got to do with any woman of that kind?]

DUCHESS OF BERWICK: Ah, what indeed, dear? That
is the point. He goes to see her continually, and stops
for hours at a time, and while he is there she is not at
home to any one. Not that many ladies call on her,
dear, but she has a great many disreputable men
friends – my own brother particularly, as I told you –
and that is what makes it so dreadful about
Windermere. We looked upon HIM as being such a
model husband, but I am afraid there is no doubt about
it. My dear nieces – you know the Saville girls, don't
you? – such nice domestic creatures – plain,
dreadfully plain, but so good – well, they're always at
the window doing fancy work, and making ugly things
for the poor, which I think so useful of them in these
dreadful socialistic days, and this terrible woman has
taken a house in Curzon Street, right opposite them –
such a respectable street, too! I don't know what
we're coming to! And they tell me that Windermere
goes there four and five times a week – they SEE
him. They can't help it – and although they never talk
scandal, they – well, of course – they remark on it to
every one. And the worst of it all is that I have been
told that this woman has got a great deal of money out
of somebody, for it seems that she came to London six
months ago without anything at all to speak of, and
now she has this charming house in Mayfair, drives
her ponies in the Park every afternoon and all – well,
all – since she has known poor dear Windermere.

[LADY WINDERMERE: Oh, I can't believe it!]

DUCHESS OF BERWICK: But it's quite true, my dear.
The whole of London knows it. That is why I felt it

was better to come and talk to you, and advise you to take Windermere away at once to Homburg or to Aix, where he'll have something to amuse him, and where you can watch him all day long. I assure you, my dear, that on several occasions after I was first married, I had to pretend to be very ill, and was obliged to drink the most unpleasant mineral waters, merely to get Berwick out of town. He was so extremely susceptible.

A WOMAN OF NO IMPORTANCE (1893)

by Oscar Wilde

HESTER WORSLEY is a young American heiress at a house party in Wrockley. She is intelligent, forthright and elegant, not at all intimidated by the intricacies of the English class system. In this scene she expresses her views about the English aristocracy to other guests.

Act II

HESTER: The English aristocracy supply us with our curiosities, Lady Caroline. They are sent over to us every summer, regularly, in the steamers, and propose to us the day after they land. As for ruins, we are trying to build up something that will last longer than brick or stone. (*Gets up to take her fan from table.*)

[LADY HUNSTANTON: What is that, dear? Ah, yes, an iron Exhibition, is it not, at that place that has the curious name?]

HESTER: (*Standing by table.*) We are trying to build up life, Lady Hunstanton, on a better, truer, purer basis than life rests on here. This sounds strange to you all, no doubt. How could it sound other than strange? You rich people in England, you don't know how you are living. How could you know? You shut out from your society the gentle and the good. You laugh at the simple and the pure. Living, as you all do, on others and by them you sneer at self-sacrifice, and if you throw bread to the poor, it is merely to keep them quiet for a season. With all your pomp and wealth and art you don't know how to live – you don't even know

that. You love the beauty that you can see and touch
and handle, the beauty that you can destroy, and do
destroy, but of the unseen beauty of life, of the unseen
beauty of a higher life, you know nothing. You have
lost life's secret. Oh, your English society seems to me
shallow, selfish, foolish. It has blinded its eyes, and
stopped its ears. It lies like a leper in purple. It sits like
a dead thing smeared with gold. It is all wrong, all
wrong.

[LADY STUTFIELD: I don't think one should know of
these things. It is not very, very nice, is it?

LADY HUNSTANTON: My dear Miss Worsley, I
thought you liked English society so much. You were
such a success in it. And you were so much admired
by the best people. I quite forget what Lord Henry
Weston said of you – but it was most complimentary,
and you know what an authority he is on beauty.]

HESTER: Lord Henry Weston! I remember him, Lady
Hunstanton. A man with a hideous smile and a hideous
past. He is asked everywhere. No dinner-party is
complete without him. What of those whose ruin is
due to him? They are outcasts. They are nameless. If
you met them in the street you would turn your head
away. I don't complain of their punishment. Let all
women who have sinned be punished.

[LADY HUNSTANTON: My dear young lady!]

HESTER: It is right that they should be punished, but
don't let them be the only ones to suffer. If a man and
woman have sinned, let them both go forth into the
desert to love or loathe each other there. Let them
both be branded. Set a mark, if you wish, on each, but

don't punish the one and let the other go free. Don't
have one law for men and another for women. You
are unjust to women in England. And till you count
what is a shame in a woman to be an infamy in a man,
you will always be unjust, and Right, that pillar of fire,
and Wrong, that pillar of cloud, will be made dim to
your eyes, or be not seen at all, or if seen, not
regarded.

ARMS AND THE MAN (1894)

by George Bernard Shaw

RAINA PETKOFF is a young Bulgarian girl who is engaged to an heroic young soldier, Sergius. In this scene, early in the play, RAINA is preparing for bed when her mother, Catherine, brings news of Sergius' success in a cavalry charge.

Act I

RAINA: I am so happy! so proud! (*She rises and walks about excitedly.*) It proves that all our ideas were real after all.

[CATHERINE: (*Indignantly.*) Our ideas real! What do you mean?]

RAINA: Our ideas of what Sergius would do. Our patriotism. Our heroic ideals. I sometimes used to doubt whether they were anything but dreams. Oh, what faithless little creatures girls are! When I buckled on Sergius's sword he looked so noble: it was treason to think of disillusion or humiliation or failure. And yet – and yet – (*She sits down again suddenly.*) Promise me you'll never tell him.

[CATHERINE: Dont ask me for promises until I know what I'm promising.]

RAINA: Well, it came into my head just as he was holding me in his arms and looking into my eyes, that perhaps we only had our heroic ideas because we are so fond of reading Byron and Pushkin, and because we were so delighted with the opera that season at

Bucharest. Real life is so seldom like that! indeed never, as far as I knew it then. (*Remorsefully.*) Only think, mother: I doubted him: I wondered whether all his heroic qualities and his soldiership might not prove mere imagination when he went into a real battle. I had an uneasy fear that he might cut a poor figure there beside all those clever officers from the Tsar's court.

[CATHERINE: A poor figure! Shame on you! The Serbs have Austrian officers who are just as clever as the Russians; but we have beaten them in every battle for all that.]

RAINA: (*Laughing and snuggling against her mother.*) Yes: I was only a prosaic little coward. Oh, to think that it was all true! that Sergius is just as splendid and noble as he looks! that the world is really a glorious world for women who can see its glory and men who can act its romance! What happiness! what unspeakable fulfilment!

THE BEAR (1894)

by Anton Chekhov
Translated by Michael Frayn
PUBLISHED BY METHUEN (ISBN 0 413 18160 X)

*In this one act comic vaudeville, POPOVA is a young
widow who has retired from the world and lives in a
darkened room in full mourning. Visited by one of her
husband's creditors, Smirnov, the pair argue and it turns
into a full-scale exchange of insults as a preamble to
falling in love. Here, Smirnov has just accused women
of being unfaithful and shallow. POPOVA responds full-
bloodedly.*

POPOVA: So who, in your opinion, if I may ask, is
    constant and true in love? Not a man, by any chance?

[SMIRNOV: A man, certainly, a man!]

POPOVA: A man! (*Gives an angry laugh.*) A man –
    constant and true in love! News to me, I must say!
    (*Heatedly.*) What right do you have to say such a
    thing? Constant and true – men? It that's what you're
    telling me then let me inform you that of all the men I
    have ever known the best was my late husband. I
    loved him passionately. I loved him with my whole
    being, as only a young and intelligent woman can love.
    I gave him my youth and happiness, my life and
    fortune; I breathed him; I prayed to him like a heathen.
    And what happened? This best of men deceived me
    most shamelessly at every step! After his death I
    found a whole drawer of his desk full of love letters.
    And while he was alive – I can scarcely bear to recall

it – he left me on my own for weeks at a time – he pursued other women in front of my eyes, he betrayed me, he squandered my money right and left, he mocked my feelings… And in spite of it all I loved him and I was true to him… And dead as he is, I remain true and constant. I have entombed myself forever within these four walls and I shall wear this mourning unto my grave…

THE SEAGULL (1898)

by Anton Chekhov
Translated by Peter Gill

PUBLISHED BY OBERON BOOKS (ISBN 1 84002 150 0)

MASHA is the daughter of the estate manager for the Sorin family and lives on the estate. Sorin's sister is a famous actress who has invited a glamorous writer, Trigorin, to stay. MASHA has fallen in love with the writer and, in this scene, speaks of her feelings. The speech also reveals that MASHA is a secret alcoholic.

Act III

MASHA: I'm telling all this to you because you're a writer and you may be able to use it. In all truth, if he had really harmed himself I don't think I could have borne it. I don't know what I would have done. But luckily I'm quite tough. I've made up my mind to tear this love out of my heart, tear it out by the roots.

[TRIGORIN: How are you going to do that?]

MASHA: I'm going to marry Medvedenko.

[TRIGORIN: The schoolmaster?]

MASHA: Yes.

[TRIGORIN: I really don't see why you have to do that.]

MASHA: Hopeless love. Years and years spent waiting. No. And after I'm married, I won't have time for love, will I? There'll be new cares for me to deal with and they'll soon displace the old ones. And it will be a change, won't it? Shall we have another?

[TRIGORIN: Don't you think you've had enough?]

MASHA: Just one more. I don't know why you're
looking at me like that. Women drink more often than
you think. But only a few women drink openly as I do.
Most of them drink secretly. Alone. Yes, they do. And
it's always vodka and brandy. (*Clinks glasses.*) In
many ways you're a simple man, aren't you? I shall be
sorry to say goodbye.

(*MASHA and Trigorin drink.*)

[TRIGORIN: I don't want to go.

MASHA: Why don't you ask her to stay?

TRIGORIN: It would do no good. She won't stay now.
I'm afraid Konstantin Gavrilovich has behaved with a
quite remarkable lack of tact. First he tries to shoot
himself and then he announces that he's going to
challenge me to a duel. He sulks. He stamps about the
place, snorting with contempt, preaching his doctrine
of new forms. I can't see why there isn't room for the
old forms and the new. But no, there's nothing for it
but the old must go, it seems. Why all this aggression?

MASHA: It's jealously. It's none of my business, any of it.]

(*Pause. Yakov crosses from left to right with suitcases.
Nina enters and stands by the window.*)

He's not very clever, my schoolteacher. But he's a
kind man. He's poor, I know, but he loves me very
much. I feel sorry for him and I feel sorry for his poor
mother, too. I wish you all good things. Don't think too
badly of me when you've left, will you? (*Shakes
Trigorin's hand warmly.*)

I'm grateful to you for all your kind attention. And you will promise to send me your books, won't you? And will you please sign them? Don't put, 'To my dear friend,' or anything like that, but simply write, 'To Marya who nobody knows and whose purpose on this earth is nothing.' Goodbye. (*She exits.*)

MAJOR BARBARA (1906)

by George Bernard Shaw

*BARBARA, a major in the Salvation Army, has to deal
with the struggle between spirituality and worldly power.
Her father is a Machiavellian millionaire, Undershaft,
who reveals that a shelter for the poor was financed by
money made immorally. BARBARA's fiancé, Adolphus
('Dolly') Cusins, engineers a situation in which some of
the moral issues are resolved and here, at the end of the
play, BARBARA explains to Adolphus how she plans to
proceed in future.*

Act III

BARBARA: Oh, if only I could get away from you and
from father and from it all! If I could have the wings
of a dove and fly away to heaven!

[CUSINS: And leave me!]

BARBARA: Yes, you, and all the other naughty
mischievous children of men. But I can't. I was happy
in the Salvation Army for a moment. I escaped from
the world into a paradise of enthusiasm and prayer and
soul saving; but the moment our money ran short, it all
came back to Bodger: it was he who saved our people:
he, and the Prince of Darkness, my papa. Undershaft
and Bodger: their hands stretch everywhere: when we
feed a starving fellow creature, it is with their bread,
because there is no other bread; when we tend the
sick, it is in the hospitals they endow; if we turn from
the churches they build, we must kneel on the stones
of the streets they pave. As long as that lasts, there is

no getting away from them. Turning our backs on
Bodger and Undershaft is turning our backs on life.

[CUSINS: I thought you were determined to turn your
back on the wicked side of life.]

BARBARA: There is no wicked side: life is all one. And
I never wanted to shirk my share in whatever evil
must be endured, whether it be sin or suffering. I wish
I could cure you of middle-class ideas, Dolly.

[CUSINS: (*Gasping.*) Middle cl–! A snub! A social snub
to me! from the daughter of a foundling!]

BARBARA: That is why I have no class, Dolly: I come
straight out of the heart of the whole people. If I were
middle-class I should turn my back on my father's
business; and we should both live in an artistic drawing
room, with you reading the reviews in one corner, and
I in the other at the piano, playing Schumann: both
very superior persons, and neither of us a bit of use.
Sooner than that, I would sweep out the guncotton
shed, or be one of Bodger's barmaids. Do you know
what would have happened if you had refused papa's
offer?

[CUSINS: I wonder!]

BARBARA: I should have given you up and married the
man who accepted it. After all, my dear old mother
has more sense than any of you. I felt like her when I
saw this place – felt that I must have it – that never,
never, never could I let it go; only she thought it was
the houses and the kitchen ranges and the linen and
china, when it was really all the human souls to be
saved: not weak souls in starved bodies, sobbing with
gratitude for a scrap of bread and treacle, but fullfed,
quarrelsome, snobbish, uppish creatures, all standing

on their little rights and dignities, and thinking that my
father ought to be greatly obliged to them for making
so much money for him – and so he ought. That is
where salvation is really wanted. My father shall
never throw it in my teeth again that my converts
were bribed with bread. (*She is transfigured.*) I have
got rid of the bribe of bread. I have got rid of the bribe
of heaven. Let God's work be done for its own sake:
the work he had to create us to do because it cannot
be done except by living men and women. When I die,
let him be in my debt, not I in his; and let me forgive
him as becomes a woman of my rank.

BLOOD WEDDING (1933)

by Federico Garcia Lorca
Translated by Gwynne Edwards

PUBLISHED BY METHUEN   (ISBN 0 413 15780 6)

This bleak and passionate tragedy, set among Spanish peasants, concerns the BRIDE who, on her wedding day, jilts her betrothed and runs away with her former lover, Leonardo. The bridegroom gives chase and both he and Leonardo are killed. In the final scene, the BRIDE returns to the bridegroom's house and confronts his mother.

Act III, Scene II

BRIDE: I came so that she could kill me, so that they could bear me away with them. (*To the Mother.*) But not with their hands; with iron hooks, with a sickle, and with a force that will break it on my bones. Leave her! I want her to know that I'm clean, that even though I'm mad they can bury me and not a single man will have looked at himself in the whiteness of my breasts.

[MOTHER: Be quiet, be quiet! What does that matter to me?]

BRIDE: Because I went off with the other one! I went! (*In anguish.*) You would have gone too. I was a woman burning, full of pain inside and out, and your son was a tiny drop of water that I hoped would give me children, land, health; but the other one was a dark river, full of branches, that brought to me the sound of its reeds and its soft song. And I was going with your son, who was like a child of cold water, and the other one sent hundreds of birds that blocked my path and

left frost on the wounds of this poor, withered woman,
this girl caressed by fire. I didn't want to, listen to me!
I didn't want to! Your son was my ambition and I
haven't deceived him, but the other one's arm dragged
me like a wave from the sea, like the butt of a mule,
and would always have dragged me, always, always,
even if I'd been an old woman and all the sons of your
son had tried to hold me down by my hair!

(*A Neighbour enters.*)

[MOTHER: She's not to blame! Nor me! (*Sarcastically.*)
So who's to blame? A weak, delicate, restless woman
who throws away a crown of orange-blossom to look
for a piece of bed warmed by another woman!]

BRIDE: Be quiet, be quiet! Take your revenge on me!
Here I am! See how soft my throat is; less effort for
you than cutting a dahlia in your garden. But no, not
that! I'm pure, as pure as a new-born child. And
strong enough to prove it to you. Light the fire. We'll
put our hands in it: you for your son; me for my body.
You'll be the first to take them out.

YERMA (1934)

by Federico Garcia Lorca
Translated by Peter Luke

PUBLISHED BY METHUEN (ISBN 0 413 15780 6)

Yerma is a peasant woman, married to Juan, and destroyed by her inability to bear her husband a child. The SECOND GIRL is newly married and sees her destiny to be a mother just as clearly as Yerma. She is talking to Yerma in this scene.

Act I, Scene II

SECOND GIRL: If you had four or five kids about the house you wouldn't be so fussy.

[YERMA: I would – however many.]

SECOND GIRL: But you haven't, any more than I have. So life's nice and peaceful.

[YERMA: Peaceful? Not for me.]

SECOND GIRL: For me it is. The only trouble is my mother never stops stuffing me with herbs and that to try and make me pregnant. And then when October comes round she drags me off to that old Saint who's supposed to give you babies if you pray hard enough. Well, she can pray as much as she likes but you won't catch me.

[YERMA: Why did you get married then?]

SECOND GIRL: Get married? Doesn't everyone? My parents wanted me out of the house. The way it's going the only ones left single will be the under-twelves.

Anyway, we were really married long before we got to the Church. It's the old people who push you into those sort of things. I'm nineteen, I hate housework and if you're always doing the things you hate what's the point of life? Is my husband any better to me now than he was before? We still do the same sort of things, don't we? Marriage is old-fashioned rubbish.

[YERMA: Shut up. Don't talk like that.]

SECOND GIRL: You think I'm barmy; the barmy girl! The crazy girl! (*Laughs.*) But the one thing life has taught me is that most people spend their lives bottled up inside their houses doing the things they hate. But I like dressing up and feeling everybody's eyes on me when I walk down the street. I please myself. I'd swim naked in the stream and ring the Church bells if I felt like it; and when I'm in the mood I'll take a drink with any man.

[YERMA: You're just a kid.]

SECOND GIRL: Maybe, but I'm not stupid! (*She laughs.*)

DONA ROSITA THE SPINSTER (1935)

By Federico Garcia Lorca
Translated by Gwynne Edwards

PUBLISHED BY METHUEN (ISBN 0 413 15780 6)

DONA ROSITA was separated from her fiancé while still a teenager. He went to America and she waited for him. Though he never returned, a marriage by proxy was arranged. In fact, though, he married someone else. Many years have passed and ROSITA, now in her forties, is explaining to her elderly aunt why she is determined never to marry.

Act III

ROSITA: (*Kneeling.*) I've become accustomed to living outside myself for many years now, thinking about things that were far away... And now that these things no longer exist, I find myself going around and around in a cold place, searching for a way out that I'll never find... I knew the truth. I knew he'd got married. A kind soul insisted on telling me, but I went on receiving his letters with an illusion full of sadness that surprised even me... If no one had said anything; if you hadn't known; if only I had known the truth, his letters and his deceit would have fed my dream as they did in the first year of his absence. But everyone knew the truth and I'd find myself picked out by a pointing finger that ridiculed the modesty of a girl soon to be married and made grotesque the fan of a girl who was still single. Each year that passed was like an intimate piece of clothing torn from my body. One day a friend gets married, and then another, and yet another, and the next day she has a son, and the son grows up and comes to show me his examination marks. Or there are new houses and new songs. And there am I, with the same trembling excitement, cutting the same carnations, looking at the same clouds. And then one day I'm out walking, and I suddenly realise I don't know anyone. Girls and boys leave me behind because I can't keep up, and one of them says: 'There's the old maid,' and another one, a good-looking boy with curly hair says, 'No one's going to fancy her again.' I hear it all and I can't protest against it. I can only go on, with a mouth full of bitterness and a great desire to run away, to take off my shoes, to rest and never move again from my corner.

[AUNT: Oh, Rosita, my child!]

ROSITA: I'm too old now. Yesterday I heard the housekeeper say that I'd still be able to marry. Never! Don't even think it! I lost that hope when I lost the man I wanted with all my blood, the man I loved…and go on loving. Everything's finished…and yet, with all my dreams destroyed, I go to bed and get up again with the terrible feeling that hope is finally dead… I want to run away, not to be able to see, to be calm, empty… Doesn't a poor woman have the right to breathe freely? And yet hope pursues me, circles around me, gnaws at me: like a dying wolf trying to sink his teeth in for the last time.

THE HOUSE OF BERNARDA ALBA (1936)

by Federico Garcia Lorca
Translated by James Graham-Lujan
& Richard L O'Connell

PUBLISHED BY NEW DIRECTIONS (ISBN 0 8112 00922)

The play tells of the repression of five daughters by a domineering woman, Bernarda Alba. The daughters' natural spirits spoil their mother's plans but their actions result in violence and death. MARTIRIO is twenty-four and here speaking to her older sister about a mutual friend. MARTIRIO is in poor health and has recently been visited by the doctor.

Act I

MARTIRIO: Her sweetheart doesn't let her go out even to the front doorstep. Before, she was gay. Now, not even powder on her face.

[AMELIA: These days a girl doesn't know whether to have a beau or not.

MARTIRIO: It's all the same.

AMELIA: The whole trouble is all these wagging tongues that won't let us live. Adelaida has probably had a bad time.]

MARTIRIO: She's afraid of our mother. Mother is the only one who knows the story of Adelaida's father and where he got his lands. Every time she comes here, Mother twists the knife in the wound. Her father killed his first wife's husband in Cuba so he could marry her himself. Then he left her there and went off with another woman who already had one daughter, and then he took up with this other girl, Adelaida's mother, and married her after his second wife died insane.

[AMELIA: But why isn't a man like that put in jail?]

MARTIRIO: Because men help each other cover up things like that and no one's able to tell on them.

[AMELIA: But Adelaida's not to blame for any of that.]

MARTIRIO: No. But history repeats itself. I can see that everything is a terrible repetition. And she'll have the same fate as her mother and grandmother – both of them wife to the man who fathered her.

[AMELIA: What an awful thing!]

MARTIRIO: It's better never to look at a man. I've been afraid of them since I was a little girl. I'd see them in the yard, yoking the oxen and lifting grain sacks, shouting and stamping, and I was always afraid to grow up for fear one of them would suddenly take me in his arms. God has made me weak and ugly and has definitely put such things away from me.

[AMELIA: Don't say that! Enrique Humanas was after you and he like you.]

MARTIRIO: That was just people's ideas! One time I stood in my nightgown at the window until daybreak because he let me know through his shepherd's little girl that he was going to come, and he didn't. It was all just talk. Then he married someone else who had more money than I.

[AMELIA: And ugly as the devil.]

MARTIRIO: What do men care about ugliness? All they care about is lands, yokes of oxen, and a submissive bitch who'll feed them.

Appendix

Biographical Notes on the Playwrights

Sophocles (495–406 BC)

Sophocles was an Athenian, born to a merchant family and, as a youth, famous for his good looks and physical grace. His artistic talents revealed themselves early and he led a boys' choir at a celebration of the Athenian military victory at Salamis in 479 BC. At the age of 28, he first competed in the City Dionysia, the annual tragic writing competition, and won first prize.

He is known to have written 120 plays, of which seven are extant. In a glittering career he won eighteen prizes at the Dionysia and never came lower than second in the competition. He also performed in many of his own plays and caused a stir with an elaborate juggling act in his own play, *Nausicaa*. As well as the theatre, Sophocles was actively involved in politics and military affairs, served as a priest and was, for a time, director of the Athenian Treasury.

The dramatic form inherited by Sophocles involved only two actors plus the Chorus. Sophocles added a third actor. He may also have been responsible for the use of painted scenery.

His *Oedipus* trilogy – *Antigone, Oedipus the King* and *Oedipus at Colonus* – is considered his greatest achievement, though the plays were not designed as a trilogy. His other extant plays are *Electra, Ajax* and *Women of Trachis.*

Euripides (480–406 BC)

Euripides is the most 'modern' of the Greek tragic writers but, in his time, was a controversial and challenging figure. He first competed in the City Dionysia in 455 BC but it was fourteen years before he won a first prize. He only won five awards in his entire career, the final one presented after his death for his masterpiece *The Bacchai*. He wrote around 92 plays, of which 11 survive.

Euripides' style was abrasive and challenging, openly critical of the status quo and disrespectful of authority. His characters have considerable psychological realism and his sympathetic depiction of women in extremis allows them a respect which was contrary to the spirit of his age.

Superstition and hypocrisy were frequent targets in his plays. Pacifism and tolerance were qualities he admired, again at odds with the Athenian audience.

His most celebrated plays are *Hippolytus, The Bacchai, The Trojan Women* and *Medea,* all anti-heroic and anti-establishment. Other plays include *Hecuba, Helen, Iphigenia in Tauris* and *Iphigenia in Aulis.*

William Shakespeare (1564–1616)

Controversy surrounds what little we know of Shakespeare's biography. Born and educated in Stratford-upon-Avon, the son of middle-class glove-maker John Shakespeare and well-born Mary Arden, Shakespeare married Anne Hathaway and sired three children – Suzannah, Hamnet and Judith. He was established in London as part of the King's Men by the early 1590s and wrote some thirty seven plays before retiring to New Place in Stratford around 1612. Shakespeare was an actor and is believed to have played roles in his own plays, among them the Ghost in *Hamlet* and Duke Senior in *As You Like It.* He wrote many of his leading roles for the King's Men's leading actor, the flamboyant Richard Burbage.

Shakespeare's works include a cycle of history plays covering English history from Richard II to Richard III; a series of Roman tragedies (*Julius Caesar, Titus Andronicus, Anthony and Cleopatra* and *Coriolanus*); a clutch of comedies including *Twelfth Night, The Merchant of Venice, The Taming of the Shrew, Much Ado About Nothing* and *As You Like It;* the celebrated tragedies *Hamlet, Macbeth, Othello* and *King Lear;* as well as plays which are less easy to categorise – bitter comedies such as *Measure for Measure* and *Troilus and Cressida* and fables of forgiveness and redemption such as *The Winter's Tale* and *The Tempest.*

He had become prosperous by the time he retired and died at the age of 54, bequeathing his wife, Anne, his second best bed – a quirky entry in his will which has given rise to fascinated speculation ever since.

John Webster (c 1580–c 1635)

TS Eliot famously described Webster as seeing 'the skull beneath the skin.' Little is known of Webster's life but he is believed to have been a student at the Middle Temple, which would explain the many legal references in his plays. By 1602 he was collaborating with other dramatists on a play for Philip Henslowe, actor and theatre manager. This collaborative effort was called *Caesar's Fall.*

Webster is best remembered for two magnificent, dark-toned tragedies – *The Duchess of Malfi* and *The White Devil* written in 1612 and 1614. In 1620 he wrote *The Devil's Law Case* and in 1621 collaborated with Thomas Middleton on *Anything for a Quiet Life.* Four years later came *The Fair Maid of the Inn,* co-written with Philip Massinger and John Ford. Around the same time he worked with Thomas Heywood on *A Cure for a Cuckold. Appius and Virginia,* a Roman tragedy, appeared some time in the late 1620s or early 1630s. It is believed that Webster died shortly afterwards, though the date is not known.

Webster is also often credited as being Shakespeare's collaborator on *The Two Noble Kinsmen* and *Henry VIII*.

William Wycherley (1640–1716)

Wycherley was born in Shropshire, the son of a farmer. He was educated in France and at Oxford, but never graduated. He entered the Inner Temple as a student of law. His first comedy, *Love in a Wood*, set in fashionable St James' Park, brought him to the favour of the Duchess of Cleveland, one of the King's mistresses. As a result, Wycherley began to move in court circles. However, this all stopped when he fell in love with and secretly married the Countess of Drogheda. Charles II had offered Wycherley the chance to educate his son, the Duke of Richmond, but when the marriage was discovered, the King withdrew the offer. Wycherley was then dropped by fashionable society. His most famous, much revived play is *The Country Wife* (1675) and his other works include *The Plain Dealer*, *The Gentleman Dancing Master* and a collection of poems.

Aphra Behn (1640–1689)

Aphra Behn's life, or such as is known of it, is as lively, colourful and spirited as her plays. Having been a professional spy for the Stuart court (code-named 'Astrea', Agent 160) she turned to writing for a living. For the first twenty years of her career she was England's sole female playwright. It has been rumoured that she was James II's mistress. She must have been largely self-educated as women at that time were barred from the universities, the Inns of Court and the Temple.

Sex and power – and the relationship between them – were key themes of Behn's work and it is tempting to believe that this came from her own experience. These subjects were considered unsuitable for a woman to think about, let alone discuss, so for many years Behn was regarded as a 'smutty' author. It was not until the twentieth century that her work began to be reconsidered and Virginia Woolf championed the revival of her reputation.

Behn's extant plays include *The Rover, The City Heiress, The Feigned Courtesans, The Lucky Chance* and *The Emperor and the Moon.* She also wrote a novel, *Orinookoo,* with an exotic Caribbean background.

William Congreve (1670–1729)

Of English birth, educated in Ireland alongside Jonathan Swift (at Kilkenny School and Trinity College Dublin), Congreve set out to pursue a career in law, but the sudden and unexpected success of his first play, at the age of 23, caused him to devote his life to writing. Following his first hit, *The Old Bachelor*, he wrote *The Double Dealer* in 1694, *Love for Love* a year later and his undoubted masterpiece, *The Way of the World*, in 1700. He had an astute and cynical eye for the misbehaviour of the fashionable society in which he moved. His one attempt at tragedy, *The Mourning Bride*, was unsuccessfully produced in 1687.

Though *The Way of the World* has survived as one of the jewels of restoration theatre, it was poorly received at the time and its comparative failure made Congreve decide to abandon the theatre. He was moderately prosperous by this time and he held a number of government posts over the next few years. He also presided over a 'salon' of the great minds of his time, including Swift, Steele, Pope and Voltaire. Romantically, he had a long (but never formalised) relationship with the celebrated actress, Mrs Bracegirdle. On his death, he was buried in Westminster Abbey.

George Farquhar (c 1677–1707)

Farquhar's life was lively but short. A spirited Irishman, born in Londonderry and educated at Trinity College Dublin, he first became a soldier and then an actor. However, during one performance he seriously wounded a fellow player in an onstage duel and gave up performing. He turned to writing instead and produced *Love and a Bottle* in 1698 at the age of 21, followed by, at almost annual intervals, by *The Constant Couple, Sir Harry Wildair, The Inconstant, The Twin Rivals* and *The Stage Coach*. His last two plays are his best – both *The Recruiting Officer* and *The Beaux Strategem* are among the most commonly revived eighteenth-century plays.

Farquhar enjoyed drink and women. Although his plays were commercially successful he had no conception of the virtues of thrift and he died in poverty – indeed, he was only able to avoid debtor's prison and write his final play, *The Beaux Stratagem*, thanks to a loan from an actor, Robert Wilks. Farquhar's wife claimed to have a greater fortune than in fact was the case – but when he discovered this, Farquhar laughed it off and always treated her with kindness and affection.

Carlo Goldoni (1707–1793)

A native of Venice, much of Goldoni's extensive theatrical output is set in that city and based on its manners and morals. Italian theatre at that date had been dominated by *commedia dell'arte* with its stock characters. Goldoni used this tradition and developed it with an acute psychological realism that informed both the 150 comedies he penned and the 100 other works, among them tragedies, satires and works of social realism. A practical man of the theatre, Goldoni was not above taking old plays and reworking them. In 1762 he moved to Paris where he was to die many years later in abject poverty.

His plays include *The Servant of Two Masters, The Fan, The Venetian Twins, Mirandolina, The Housekeeper, The Coffee Shop* and *The Tyrants.*

Oliver Goldsmith (1730–1774)

Goldsmith is perhaps unique in writing acknowledged masterpieces in three different literary media – of prose, poetry and drama. The second son of an Irish clergyman, he studied at Trinity College Dublin and later obtained a medical degree in Europe. He travelled widely in France, Switzerland and Italy, finally returning to London in a state of destitution. He supported himself with some difficulty as a physician, an usher and a hack writer on magazines. In 1758 he published a well-received translation of *The Memoirs of a Protestant*, and after this his public profile began to rise. He became a friend of Dr Johnson and contributed to many magazines as well as writing the celebrated novel, *The Vicar of Wakefield* (1766). He wrote lives of Voltaire, Parnell and Bolingbroke and turned his hand to playwriting with *The Good Natured Man,* which was rejected by the leading actor of the day, David Garrick, though subsequently performed at Covent Garden. This he followed with *She Stoops to Conquer* (1773), his masterpiece. The poem, *The Deserted Village* appeared in 1770. Goldsmith makes several appearances in Boswell's famous *Life of Johnson.*

Richard Brinsley Sheridan (1751–1816)

The son of an Irish actor-manager, Sheridan learned early that the theatre offered, at best, a precarious living. It was also considered ungentlemanly. Sheridan was sent to Harrow

School where he was unhappy, being regarded as a dunce. Joining his family in Bath, however, he soon began writing skits for the newspapers and satirical pamphlets. He eloped with Eliza Linley, a beautiful young singer, whom he 'married' illegally abroad, and over whom he fought at least two duels with her overbearing admirer, an army captain. Sheridan's father split up the pair and sent Richard to study law, but love triumphed and in 1773 Richard married Eliza legally.

By now, though, he was very short of money and wrote *The Rivals* very quickly as a means to generate some income. It was hugely successful and the 24 year old writer became the darling of the fashionable set. He followed up his success with *St Patrick's Day*, *The Duenna* and *A Trip to Scarborough,* before producing his most celebrated play *The School for Scandal* in 1777.

Though his income soared, so too did his expenditure and he became dogged by financial difficulties. He bought the lease on Drury Lane Theatre, which he managed for some years, producing other plays such as *The Critic* and *Pizarro.* Still living well beyond his means, he entered Parliament in 1780, and subsequently worked for the Treasury. However, by 1809, a combination of bad theatre management and high living (despite the dowry brought him by his second wife, Esther, after Eliza's death) caused his financial world to crumble around him and he died in poverty despite the sincere efforts of his friends. In these last years, too, he may have suffered from a brain disease.

Henrik Ibsen (1828–1906)

The Norwegian playwright often called the 'father of modern drama' began his career writing verse dramas on historical subjects, many of which were never performed. He first came to international attention with two verse plays designed to be read rather than performed – *Brand* and *Peer Gynt*

(1867). As Ibsen steadily became more successful he moved south, spending much time in Italy, though his plays were always set in the cold, bleak, Norwegian landscapes of his youth and early manhood. Abandoning his historical subjects after *Emperor and Galilean* (1872), he turned to social realism and well-turned dramas in which the past comes back to haunt characters and provoking a crisis in the present. He dealt with social problems in such plays as *Pillars of the Community* and *An Enemy of the People* before he began to concentrate on character and aberrant psychology. This, coupled with themes and subjects that were regarded by his society as difficult and shocking, made him a controversial figure with such plays (now acknowledged as masterpieces) as *A Doll's House* (1879), *Ghosts* (1881), *Rosmersholm* (1886), *Hedda Gabler* (1890) and *The Master Builder* (1893).

In his late plays, such as *When We Dead Awaken* and *John Gabriel Borkman*, he explored overt symbolism and returned to the poetic feel, if not the language, of his earlier work. Long described as a champion of women's rights, Ibsen himself refuted this, saying that he preferred to be considered a champion of human rights.

Oscar Wilde (1854–1900)

The splendidly named Oscar Fingal O'Flahertie Wills Wilde was born in Dublin to a society doctor (whose reputation was blackened by a sexual scandal) and an extraordinary mother who was both a popular political writer and the hostess of a dazzling literary salon. Wilde was brilliant intellectually and began to forge a flamboyant reputation while at Oxford University as a leader of the 'aesthetic' movement. A great self publicist, Wilde established his outrageous reputation by well-reported bon mots. When entering America to give a lecture tour he was stopped at customs and famously said, 'I have nothing to declare except my genius.' Wilde later said that his tragedy was that he had put his genius into his life and only his talent into his writings.

His life was certainly eventful. He met and began a liaison with Lord Alfred ('Bosie') Douglas while at Oxford and together, despite Wilde's marriage to the intelligent and sensitive Constance, Wilde and the shallow, temperamental Douglas, lived quite openly among the homosexual Victorian demi-monde – which Wilde described as 'feasting with panthers'.

Meanwhile, Wilde established his literary credentials with a 'shocking' novel, *The Picture of Dorian Gray* (1890), a collection of exquisite fairy tales including *The Happy Prince* and *The Selfish Giant*, a collection of poems and several short stories, including *Lord Arthur Savile's Crime.* Wilde's early plays were unremarkable and unsuccessful melodramas (*The Duchess of Padua, Vera*) but in 1892 *Lady Windermere's Fan* was a huge success, to be followed over the next three years by *An Ideal Husband, A Woman of No Importance, Salomé* (written in French and banned in Britain) and *The Importance of Being Earnest.*

Bosie's father, the slightly mad Marquess of Queensbury, objected to Wilde's friendship with his son and left a card at Wilde's club accusing Wilde of 'posing as a sodomite', homosexuality being a criminal offence. At Bosie's insistence, Wilde sued Queensbury for libel, lost the case, was prosecuted, convicted and sentenced to two years hard labour. Most of this time he spent in Reading Gaol where his health collapsed. On release in 1897, he published *The Ballad of Reading Gaol* and went to live in Europe, being briefly and unsuccessfully reunited with Bosie. He died in Paris, not long after commenting to his doctor that the rather violent magenta wallpaper was killing him – 'one of us has got to go'.

George Bernard Shaw (1856–1950)

The long and prolific career of Ireland's most famous vegetarian produced a vast number of plays and essays and he lived long enough to see a number of his plays very successfully filmed. Born in Dublin to unhappily married parents, Shaw had moved to London by the time he was 20 and was soon writing articles and essays on socialism and social issues. He wrote music, art and literary criticism alongside his career as a playwright and was a great supporter of Ibsen and the new ideas in society and the theatre as the nineteenth century became the twentieth. Famously cranky and eccentric, he claimed to despise Shakespeare ('I would like to dig him up and throw stones at him') and refused to conform to accepted rules of spelling and punctuation. He was an influential figure in the Fabian Society.

His first play *Widower's Houses* (1893) was poorly received, but he was a tireless worker and over the next ten years a number of plays followed which include some of his best-loved titles – *Arms and the Man, Caesar and Cleopatra, You Never Can Tell, The Devil's Disciple, Mrs Warren's Profession* and *Man and Superman.* In the twentieth century, highlights include *Major Barbara* (1905), *Pygmalion* (1913), *Heartbreak House* (1920), *Saint Joan* (1923) and *The Apple Cart* (1929). After this his output slowed down and of his later plays only *The Millionairess* is much performed today.

Shaw won the Nobel Prize in 1925, was a strict teetotaller, had a happy marriage lasting forty-five years and died at the age of 94 as independent as ever.

Anton Chekhov (1860–1904)

Along with Ibsen, the most influential playwright in the development of naturalism as a style, Chekhov trained as a doctor in medicine. He began writing short stories to supplement his income and published several collections. His stories include *The Lady with the Lapdog* (1899), *Ward 6* (1892) and *About Love* (1898).

His first successful play was *Ivanov* (1887), after which he wrote a number of short 'vaudevilles' including *The Bear, The Proposal* and *The Dangers of Smoking*. His reputation, however, rests on his four final plays which were produced at the Moscow Arts Theatre under the direction of the legendary Konstantin Stanislavski. These plays are *The Seagull* (1896), *Uncle Vanya* (1900), *Three Sisters* (1901) and *The Cherry Orchard* (1904).

After a long affair, Chekhov married the actress Olga Knipper in 1901. They divided their time between Moscow and a modest dacha outside Yalta. Chekhov continued to work as a doctor and it has often been said that his written work shows a medical man's clinical eye for the foibles of human behaviour. A heavy smoker, he died of consumption.

Federico Garcia Lorca (1898–1936)

Born near Granada in Southern Spain, Lorca was immersed in the language and traditions of his Andalucian homeland. From an early age he was an accomplished pianist and poet, and his work showed signs of erotic angst and anticlerical fury. Lorca was homosexual and his sense of being an outcast, coupled with his feeling for the traditions of his heritage, created an inner tension that was seen in much of his poetry. He moved to Madrid and become part of a circle which included artists Salvador Dali and filmmaker Luis Buñuel. His book of gypsy poems *Romancero Gitano* catapulted him to fame, which he rejected, preferring to move to New York where he wrote a film script, *Trip to the Moon*, further poetry and an explicitly homosexual play *The Audience*. In 1932, he was appointed director of Madrid University's travelling theatre company and began writing the plays for which he is remembered – *Blood Wedding, Yerma, The House of Bernarda Alba* and *Dona Rosita the Spinster*.

In 1936 the Spanish Civil War began. Flamboyant, intellectually acute, outspoken and openly homosexual, Lorca was a natural target for the Fascists, who murdered him.

Acknowledgements

For permission to reprint the copyright material in the publication we make grateful acknowledgement to the following authors, publishers and executors:

Chekhov, Anton *The Bear* (translated by Michael Frayn), *The Cherry Orchard, The Seagull* (two extracts included) (translated by Peter Gill) used by permission of Meuthen Publishing.

Euripides *Bacchai* (translated by Colin Teevan), *Medea* (two extracts included) (translated by Alistair Elliot) used by permission of Oberon Books.

Goldoni, Carlo *Don Juan* (two extracts included), *Friends and Lovers* (three extracts included), *The Housekeeper* (translated by Robert David MacDonald) used by permission of Oberon Books.

Ibsen, Henrik *A Doll's House* (translated by Michael Meyer) used by permission of Meuthen Publishing.

Ibsen, Henrik *Brand* (two extracts included) (translated and adapted by Robert David MacDonald)

Lorca, Federico Garcia *Blood Wedding* (translated by Gwynne Edwards), *Dona Rosita the Spinster* (translated by Gwynne Edwards), *Yerma* (translated by Peter Luke), *The House of Bernarda Alba* (two extracts included) (translated by James Graham-Lujan & Richard L O'Connell) used by permission of William Peter Kosmas and New Directions Publishing.

Shaw, George Bernard *Arms and the Man, Candida, Major Barbara, Mrs Warren's Profession, You Never Can Tell, The Man of Destiny, Caesar and Cleopatra* (translated by L Dowdeswell) used by permission of The Society of Authors.

Sophocles *Ajax* (two extracts included) (translated by James Kerr), *Antigone* (three extracts included) (translated by Declan Donnellan), *Philoctetes* (translated by Keith Dewhurst) used by permission of Oberon Books.